Ghosts of Hertfordshire

Other titles in this series include:

GHOSTS OF BERKSHIRE
Ian McLoughlin

CHESHIRE GHOSTS & LEGENDS
Frederick Woods

DERBYSHIRE GHOSTS & LEGENDS
David Bell

GHOSTS OF EAST ANGLIA
Harold Mills-West

LEICESTERSHIRE GHOSTS & LEGENDS
David Bell

**GHOSTS & LEGENDS OF LINCOLNSHIRE &
THE FEN COUNTRY**
Polly Howat

NORFOLK GHOSTS & LEGENDS
Polly Howat

NORTHAMPTONSHIRE GHOSTS & LEGENDS
Marian Pipe

**GHOSTS & LEGENDS OF STAFFORDSHIRE &
THE BLACK COUNTRY**
David Bell

GHOSTS OF SURREY
John Janaway

SUSSEX GHOSTS AND LEGENDS
Tony Wales

Ghosts
of
Hertfordshire

Betty Puttick

COUNTRYSIDE BOOKS
NEWBURY, BERKSHIRE

First Published 1994
© Betty Puttick 1994

Countryside Books
3 Catherine Road
Newbury, Berkshire

ISBN 1 85306 292 8

Cover illustration by Colin Doggett

Produced through MRM Associates Ltd., Reading
Typeset by Paragon Typesetters, Clwyd
Printed in England

To Richard
without whom this book wouldn't have
had a ghost of a chance

Ghosts
of
Hertfordshire

Contents

Introduction   9

1. St Albans' Haunted Abbey   11

2. The Valley of the Nightingales   17

3. Abbots Langley's Restless Spirit   23

4. The Ghosts of Knebworth   28

5. A King's Mistress Still Lingers   33

6. The Wicked Lady of Markyate   39

7. The Ghostly Monk of Ayot St Lawrence   45

8. The Grey Lady of Bishops Stortford   48

9. Ghosts of the Wayside   54

10. Little Boy Lost, Part 1   61

11. Little Boy Lost, Part 2   68

12. The Strange Will of Henry Trigg   73

13. A Ghost to the Rescue   78

14. The Haunting of Minsden Chapel   82

15. The Return of The Saint   86

16. '. . . And Battles Long Ago'   91

17. Last Post for a Villain   96

18. The Death of a Witch   99

19. Ghosts of Old St Albans   103

20. The Watford Hauntings   108

21. Stranger on a Train   115

22. A Ghost at the Grocers   118

Introduction

EVERYBODY is interested in ghosts, even if they don't believe in them. But what are they? There are any number of answers to that question, as any book of ghost stories illustrates.

What comparison can there be between a sighting of Catherine Howard as she runs screaming down the Haunted Gallery at Hampton Court to plead for her life, and a pub poltergeist who mischievously turns lights on and off, and hides the landlord's keys? And medieval knights, grey ladies and monks are ghosts, but not the same at all as a dear friend who unaccountably turns up at your bedside one night when, unknown to you, he has just died on the other side of the world.

These are just some of the aspects of the paranormal that people have experienced, and those who dismiss them as superstitious nonsense are ignoring the vast bulk of evidence.

But ghosts pose questions difficult to answer. Some hauntings seem no more than a shadowy replay of the past that we view rather like an old film.

Other ghosts inspire less comfortable emotions. Why do they cling to a world they should have left behind? Why are some mischievous or malevolent towards the living, and others apparently able to offer a helping hand at a vital moment?

I cannot remember when I wasn't interested in ghosts and hauntings of every kind. I saw my first ghost when I was about four, and woke in the night at my granny's house to see a stranger sitting on my bed. He looked like my father, but he wasn't my father, yet his smile was so loving and familiar that I was not afraid.

9

As I held out my arms towards him he stood up, and just disappeared. It was then that I became afraid, and ran to my parents' bed and climbed in beside my mother. I told no one what had happened, and later, looking at a portrait of my grandfather, who died before I was born, I realised who he was.

I have had several paranormal experiences over the years, and I find many people I meet have their own ghost story to tell. I have interviewed people living in haunted places, and written about their experiences for magazines; some of these stories appear in this book.

Books on haunted Great Britain generally have little to say about Hertfordshire, and yet in this county we have a wealth of interesting hauntings. We certainly have our fair share of monks, Roman soldiers and grey ladies, and more unique, we have a highwaywoman and a saint in all his glory who appeared to a child.

Pubs and shops seem to be favourite venues for paranormal activity, but apart from stately homes, I have found few ordinary houses that are haunted. Perhaps yours has a resident that is not of this world? If so, I'd love to hear about it.

I am very grateful to all those who shared their experiences and knowledge with me so generously and the staff of many Hertfordshire libraries and museums, especially Hertfordshire Local Studies Library, Hertford, Lytton Enterprises Ltd., National Westminster Bank Ltd., Stevenage, and Watford Theatre, all of whom helped me with my enquiries.

Special thanks to Rev B.K. Andrews, Albert Fiedler, Jimmy Perry, Basil Saville, Muriel Thresher, and W.J. Wright.

Betty Puttick
St Albans 1994

1

St Albans' Haunted Abbey

IT was a crisp, cold Christmas Eve as a 16 year old youth made his way up the hill towards the great Norman Abbey, standing serene in the moonlight, dominating the city of St Albans as it had for hundreds of years.

On this special night of the year people should have been flocking there for the Christmas Midnight Mass as the bells pealed out the age-old summons to celebrate the birth of Christ. But the Abbey was dark and silent, the twelve huge bells removed from the belfry, for it was 1944, England was at war, and the young man who let himself in through a side door was there as one of a team of fire-watchers. It was their job to spend the night in the Abbey in case of fire bombs, and to make a regular check of the whole building and the fire-fighting equipment. Nights like this, with what people called a 'bomber's moon', required extra vigilance.

There was no sound but his own echoing footsteps on the stone-flagged floor as Basil Saville made his way through the vast dark shadowy building to the vestry. He walked confidently for, as he had been a chorister, the Abbey was a familiar place to him, but when he discovered that no other fire-watcher had arrived, he had to admit that the thought of guarding this historic edifice on his own was a daunting prospect.

But it had to be done, so when no one else came, he set off on the regular tour of the building. It was cold and frosty outside, but the Abbey seemed even colder, with that deep penetrating chill of old churches, and the moonlight filtering faintly through the windows made the shadows even deeper.

Basil felt uneasy, something wasn't quite as it should be, and he tried to shrug off a growing feeling that although his regulation hooded torch revealed nothing untoward, he was not alone in that ancient holy place.

He followed his usual route through the Abbey, checking the water containers, stirrup pumps and hoses as he went, until he reached the Saint's Chapel where the Shrine of Saint Alban stands, and an early 15th century watching chamber from which monks used to keep a vigilant eye on pilgrims visiting the martyr's shrine.

The feeling that he too, was being watched was very strong now, and as Basil shone his torch high up into the watching chamber he felt the hairs on the back of his neck rise as he thought he could glimpse two hooded figures. He called out, then climbed the rickety old staircase up to the loft, but his torch revealed no intruders and he knew no one could have passed him. His heart beat faster as he noticed two monks' habits lying there on the floor, but Basil tried to reassure himself that they must have been used for some theatrical production, although he could not recall anything of the kind.

He was relieved to reach the blacked out Lady Chapel where at last it was possible to switch on some light, and he sat for a while trying to collect his thoughts, conscious of the lonely emptiness around him, then continued his patrol.

On his way to the twisting staircase which led to the roof he almost fell against one of the Abbey's 12 great bells which had been stored on the ground floor for the duration of the war. But as he climbed into the upper regions above the nave he all but lost his balance as suddenly a bell began to toll in the belfry. How could this be happening? Hadn't he nearly tripped over one of the bells down below? And yet the steady tolling went on, so summoning his courage he opened the belfry door as the sound died away and found, as he knew he would, that there were no bells hanging there.

The tolling had stopped and, confused and at a loss to understand his extraordinary experiences, Basil climbed out on to the roof of the tower, standing there in the moonlight, grateful for the cold fresh air on his face.

But the events of that strange Christmas night were not yet over. As he started back down the stairs, the organ began to play and looking towards the organ loft he saw a candle flickering by the console but could not see the organist. Instinctively he called out the fire-watcher's familiar warning – 'Put that light out' – and moved to get a better view.

There was no one seated at the organ and yet, from his vantage point above, Basil could see the pages of a book of music turning, and the organ keys being depressed by unseen fingers. Then suddenly from the direction of the high altar came a glorious burst of singing.

Hardly knowing what he was doing, Basil hurried down the stairs and through the Abbey towards the choir stalls. The music had stopped now, but as he looked towards the high altar he saw a magnificent sight. A procession of monks with their abbot, all holding candles, were leaving the high altar and passing through the screen doors into the Saint's Chapel. The doors closed behind them, and Basil followed to the chapel, only to find it empty and in darkness. He ran back and climbed up to the organ loft and, in the light of his torch, found a spent candle and a book of music. Here at least was some tangible evidence that he had not imagined the whole extraordinary experience.

The book was quite large, with plain black covers and yellowing manuscript pages. Opening it he read the title, *Albanus Mass* by Robert Fayrfax.

Back in the vestry, he was relieved to find his fellow fire-watcher had arrived. The other man had apparently heard and seen nothing, and together they went round the Abbey again, as Basil told his companion about the strange events he had witnessed. But when they reached the organ loft the used candle he had seen was no longer there, and the two monks' habits had disappeared from the floor of the watching loft.

Had it all been a dream? But after all these years the powerful impression of that wartime Christmas Eve remains with him.

'I was stunned by it – overwhelmed,' he recently told me. 'I'm not psychic or anything like that,' he added, 'and I've never seen anything like it either before or since. People may not believe me, but I know it happened.'

He wrote down his experience soon afterwards, while it was all fresh in his mind, but thinking people would not believe him, he kept it locked away in his memory and told no one. Then in 1982 he saw that the *Evening Post-Echo* were asking their readers for Christmas stories, so he sent them what he had written all those years ago, and they published it.

But although Basil Saville's experience may have been unique, this was not the first time that the apparently empty Abbey has echoed to the night music of an unseen choir.

W.B. Gerish, a local historian, who wrote about Hertfordshire ghost stories in the early part of this century, recalled a phantom organist who was sometimes heard playing 'heavenly music' on the Abbey organ in the middle of the night. And over the years there have been reports of sightings of Benedictine monks in and around the Abbey, figures which appear quite real only to disappear disconcertingly through walls or closed doors.

For hundreds of years the Abbey was a great Benedictine ecclesiastical establishment and seat of learning. Is it surprising that shadows of the past should linger for those able to see them or that in some strange time-warp the monks of long ago still sing the mass Robert Fayrfax wrote especially for their Abbey?

Fayrfax was organist and director of the Abbey choir at the beginning of the 16th century, and he became a great man in the musical world of his day. *The Oxford Companion to Music* refers to him as the 'prime musician of the nation', and after he became Master of the King's Musick one of the highlights of his life must surely have been when he accompanied Henry VIII to France to the Field of the Cloth of Gold, where he led the royal singers.

Fayrfax died in October 1521, and about a year before the 400th anniversary of his death, a copy of his *Albanus Mass* in the old medieval notation was discovered. It was hundreds of years since it had been performed but the fortunate coincidence inspired the Abbey organist, Willie Luttmann, to transcribe it and on October 30th 1921 it was performed at a commemorative concert at the Abbey.

The morning after the concert Mr Frank Drakard of Harpenden had some business with Canon Glossop, who lived in Romeland House, close by the Abbey, and some years ago he told me of their conversation.

'Did you enjoy the Fayrfax music last night, Canon?' 'Yes' replied the Canon, 'but you know, Drakard, I had heard it before.'

Surprised, Mr Drakard asked, 'Do you mean when they were practising?'

'No,' said the Canon, 'I have heard it in the middle of the night on more than one occasion. The first time was when I was returning home very late, and I got one of my daughters up also and we went out of doors and listened to it. When I heard it in the Abbey last night, I recognised it. I also know there was no human choir in the Abbey at the times we heard it in the night.'

'Knowing Canon Glossop as I did for a most level-headed and matter-of-fact man,' added Mr Drakard, 'I absolutely believed him.'

Dr Elsie Toms, St Albans historian, was told by Canon Glossop's daughter that one night she got out of bed to fetch a drink for a young relative who was staying with them. She heard the sound of men's voices singing in the street outside, but when she looked out of the window there was nothing to see.

She told her father, who was working late in his study, and when they both went outside the unseen procession of singers appeared to pass by and continue towards the Abbey only a stone's throw away. The Abbey gate was locked so they could not follow, but the sound went on as if the singers had entered the Abbey by the main entrance.

From time to time other people have heard music as they passed the Abbey late at night. One local resident told me that when she was a young girl in 1938 she and a friend passed by the Abbey in the late evening, and hearing 'really wonderful' music they peeped inside. But when they found the building dark and empty, they were afraid and hurried off home as fast as possible!

But as ghost stories go, the heavenly choir of St Albans Abbey is charming rather than alarming. Long may they sing.

2

The Valley of the Nightingales

HARPENDEN is a delightful little country town that many of its inhabitants like to refer to as The Village, despite the increasing development in some of its outlying districts. It has a large common with a cricket ground and golf course, and Rothamsted Park, all close to the wide main thoroughfare, and the many trees and green spaces between the shopping areas give it a rural charm. Many of the picturesque houses and inns date back centuries, and several have ghostly associations.

After a busy night in the bar of the old Cross Keys public house in Harpenden, the relief manager locked up and switched off the lights, ready for a good night's rest. He settled down, and was soon peacefully asleep as the traffic on the road outside dwindled to an occasional passing car, and the ancient building stood dreaming in the quiet of the midnight hours.

But the relief manager's slumbers were soon disturbed, and at first he could not imagine what had wakened him. He sat up in bed listening, his senses alert for anything unusual, then after a minute or two he heard it – a low murmur of voices coming from the main bar.

Silently he slipped out of bed and without switching on the light he crept quietly downstairs, praying that the creaky old stairs would not give warning of his presence to any burglar. His heart was thudding as he wondered what he would do if there were several of them. After all, what sensible burglar would go about his business talking to himself? He paused at the door to the bar, gently eased it open slightly and looked in.

The bar was in darkness except for the light from the street lamp outside, but there was just enough illumination for him to see the source of those soft murmuring voices. Three figures were sitting crouched over one of the bar tables, and as the relief manager opened the door wider, three heads turned in his direction, causing him to gasp in sheer horror and disbelief.

The faces were ghastly, shining with a greenish pallor in the street lamp's light; he could see that they had shaven heads and were wearing dark heavy robes. His mind reeled at the realisation that he was looking at three medieval monks, there in the bar where only a couple of hours before he had been laughing and pulling pints of ale for the pub's friendly regulars.

For a moment time stood still as, his mouth dry with fear, he stared at the uncanny scene before him, then he slammed the bar door shut, ran back up the stairs, locked his bedroom door, and pulled the bedclothes over his head. And for the rest of his time at the Cross Keys until the manager, Mr J. Rankin, returned from holiday, nothing would have induced him to go down to the bar again after closing time.

Similar sightings of monks in the oldest part of the Cross Keys had been reported before this episode which happened around 1960.

A guest house belonging to Westminster Abbey existed on the site in the 13th century, and the part of the pub which now houses the main bar was built in the 16th century, various additions following in the 17th and 18th centuries. Today the bar of the Cross Keys has the brass insignia of two crossed keys sunk into the floor. It is a comfortable, delightful old place full of atmosphere, but it was in this bar that in 1968 something else rather odd occurred after closing time as the landlord, Mr Johnson, and his wife were clearing up after a busy Sunday lunchtime.

Hearing a loud rumbling noise coming from the bar, they went to investigate, and to their surprise they found the extra large ash-tray, usually housed on the bar counter, was spinning like a top. Gradually it slowed down, finally subsiding to a noisy halt as they looked at it, completely at a loss to imagine what could have caused such a thing to happen. No one else was there at the time, and neither heavy traffic nor aircraft could have produced sufficient vibration to disturb the ash-tray. In any case, it was difficult to imagine what could have made such a heavy object weighing two to three pounds spin like that.

There was also the curious case of the tartan skirt, reported by Eric Rees in his booklet *My Local History*.

Mrs Brenda Johnson was entitled to wear the ancient Bruce tartan, and she was particularly fond of a skirt she owned in this material. So it was with some distress that she found one day that the skirt had unaccountably disappeared from her wardrobe. Despite a thorough search of the premises from top to bottom, the skirt was nowhere to be found, and she was obliged to accept that it appeared to have gone for good.

So it was amazing when about three months later she opened her wardrobe to get something out and found the skirt hanging from the rail just as if it had been there all the time. Then as she looked the skirt began to move, and she watched it slowly slide off the hanger and fall in a heap on the floor!

Another time the Johnsons were in their bedroom at the Cross Keys getting ready for an evening out. Mrs Johnson brushed her husband's jacket, and laid the clothes brush down on the bed. Mr Johnson, who was taking his hat out of a hat box, turned to pick up the brush, and found that it just wasn't there. Somehow the brush had completely disappeared. It could not possibly have fallen off the bed, but nevertheless they both had a good look round and there was no doubt about it. Impossible or not, the brush had vanished!

But just like the episode of the disappearing skirt, there was a sequel. Three days later, they found the brush placed in a conspicuous position on the bedroom floor by the fireplace, where it could not be missed.

The disappearance and reappearance of personal possessions is the sort of paranormal conjuring trick the occupants of haunted houses sometimes experience, and in some cases, 'apports', objects which appear unexpectedly, are completely unfamiliar to the recipient. It seems bizarre to imagine the ghosts of long dead monks playing mischievous jokes on the inhabitants of the Cross Keys pub. Could the cosy old inn perhaps be harbouring yet another ghost?

Other buildings in Harpenden have their ghostly visitations.

Rose Cottage, between shops in the High Street, was hastily abandoned a few years ago by three young men living there who were alarmed by ghostly noises in the night. The cottage is said to be haunted by an 18 year old girl who went to London in the 17th century to seek her fortune, but returned home in shame to give birth to her illegitimate baby at her parents' home, Rose Cottage. In her distress she killed her child, and then committed suicide, and since then has been seen in her nightdress searching the cottage for her baby, said to be buried in the basement.

The Silver Cup public house, a 17th century building near the Common, is haunted by a lady in grey, who was seen by the landlord, Roy Mills, in December 1985.

'Although I don't believe in ghosts, I have seen her walk

straight through a closed door,' he told the local *Review This Weekend*. 'I was stone cold sober when I went out of the office upstairs to go to the bedroom. There was this lady with her hair pulled back, wearing grey. She smiled at me, and then walked through a door.'

And in a cottage behind the Silver Cup, a young boy told his mother about the ghost of a soldier who came into his bedroom. His description fitted a First World War private, and when his mother talked about it to her neighbours, she was told that a 19 year old soldier, killed in that war, had previously lived in her cottage, and occupied the same bedroom as her son.

Many people have found Harpenden Hall a place of strange noises and alarming sensations, and I have heard of cleaners who refuse to work at the hall on their own. Someone who used to work there told me that she was getting something out of a cupboard one day when she had the distinct feeling that someone was behind her. She saw nothing when she turned round, but was conscious of sudden intense cold, and was overcome by a sensation of sheer terror.

Fortunately children seem to take any ghostly figure they may encounter in quite a matter-of-fact way, such as the small girl who wandered off up the stairs at Harpenden Hall one day and came back to tell her mother, 'Mummy, there's a funny lady up there in a long dress, and she's got no feet'.

Hagdell is a very evocative name which appears on old Harpenden maps, and marks a dell in one of the fields at Rothamsted where the legendary Ann Weatherhead lived in time gone by. Agdell Path which runs by the field from Pimlico Place to Agdell Cottage, Hatching Green, was a place to avoid after dark as this was Ann's beat, and no one cared to meet her menacing phantom. She has also been seen between Hatching Green and

Rothamsted Manor, and even on Harpenden Common nearby.

According to Arthur Mee's *Hertfordshire,* Harpenden means Valley of the Nightingales. It's a delightful name for one of Hertfordshire's most charming places, but apparently even the song of the nightingale has not driven all the shadows of the past away from Harpenden.

3

Abbots Langley's Restless Spirit

THE charming old village of Abbots Langley has one unique claim to fame. It is the birthplace of the only Englishman to become Pope.

Nicholas Breakspear was born there, a poor boy whose father joined the monastery at St Albans, leaving his son to his own devices. Nicholas also attempted to enter the monastery, but was rejected by the Abbot. It says a great deal for his character that in spite of his discouraging experience, Nicholas joined the Abbey of Avignon and rose to become its Abbot. After an exceptional career, he became a cardinal and ultimately Pope Adrian IV in 1154, when the self-same Abbot of St Albans who had rejected him was there to do him homage!

But it was with another Abbots Langley resident in mind that I visited the village while researching this book. The graveyard of St Lawrence's ancient church was billowing with drifts of cow parsley and moon daisies, the gravestones emerging rocklike from the foam, and it was not hard to imagine the wraith of Mary Ann Treble, a pale phantom in her shroud, wafting through on the way from the vicarage to her grave.

Mystery surrounds Mary Ann Treble, and the manner of her death. Why did she return to haunt St Lawrence's vicarage, the church and the churchyard? Local folklore hints darkly that Mary Ann's death was not a natural one, and the finger of suspicion pointed at Mrs Parnell, the then vicar's wife, whom public opinion decided was somehow involved. Mary Ann was a housekeeper or a servant at St Lawrence's vicarage before the First World War. The accepted theory locally was that she was badly treated by Mrs Parnell, and that she may have been murdered or committed suicide. One account says that Mary Ann died after being given 'a good shaking' because she would not get out of bed one morning after complaining of feeling unwell.

What is certain is that Mary Ann did not rest easy in her grave. After her death there were several recorded sightings of her ghost walking from the nearby vicarage to her grave in the churchyard. She was also seen in her old bedroom at the vicarage, looking out of the window, and at the same time, people living in the cottages on the opposite side of the road saw and recognised Mary Ann at the window.

The fireplace in the room she had occupied became mysteriously damaged and had to be repaired several times, and according to Peter Underwood in his *Gazetteer of British Ghosts,* a local builder who was called in to do some work assured the then vicar that it was little use repairing the fireplace as it would soon fall out again, and so it proved.

'Ann died a horrible death in this room and the place will never be free of her,' said the builder.

In an attempt to find a more down-to-earth reason for the damage to the fireplace, the vicar called in a surveyor who blamed bad workmanship, but after more repairs, just as the builder had predicted, the same thing happened again.

Traditionally, Hallowtide is a time when the veil between this world and the next is at its thinnest, and spirits of the dead are most likely to revisit their former environment. On several occasions it has been on All Souls Day that the ghost of Mary Ann has been most active, and it was on that day that a former curate once saw the ghost of a woman in the church during Mass, who then disappeared before his eyes. His description of her fitted Mary Ann Treble, and when he went back to the vicarage with the vicar after the service, they found the fireplace in the haunted bedroom freshly cracked.

On All Souls Day in the following year the ghost again appeared among the congregation, and this time it was thought advisable that the Bishop of St Albans, the Rev Michael Furse, should be told. With due ceremony he conducted the traditional service of exorcism in the vicarage, and for a time this seemed to have a calming effect on Abbots Langley's restless spirit. But not entirely. There were 'unaccountable noises' in what had been Mary Ann's room at the vicarage, and the then vicar's wife thought it best to keep the door locked.

Again, another curate alone in the church, kneeling at prayer late on the evening of a subsequent All Souls Day, heard footsteps approaching, and distinctly felt clothing brush his face as they passed by, although he saw nothing.

I was curious to know if Mary Ann had made her presence felt in more recent times. The Rev B.K. Andrews, the present vicar of Abbots Langley, told me that there is now a fireplace in only one bedroom at the vicarage, and this has remained undamaged since he came to the parish in 1979.

Regarding the manner of Mary Ann's death, he says, 'I conducted the funeral of the sister of a woman who had worked at the vicarage with Mary Ann Treble. The oral tradition which she had handed down was that Mary Ann had fallen down the stairs and died as a result of that accident, possibly of pneumonia. She may have been pushed, but my source of information gave no indication that this was so, nor that it was an act of suicide.'

So are the local theories that Mrs Parnell treated Mary

Ann badly, overworked her or prevented proper treatment being given to her when she became ill, nothing more than gossip and supposition? It seems unlikely that we shall ever know the whole story.

But soon after the Rev Andrews and his wife moved into the vicarage in 1979, two interesting things happened.

'We had a battery powered toothbrush which stood on our wash basin,' the vicar told me. 'One evening when coming to bed, we heard, and then saw that it was vibrating. Neither of us had switched it on. On another occasion I went downstairs to the kitchen, after having gone to bed, and found the electric kettle was boiling. Again, neither my wife nor I had switched the kettle on.

'These incidents might be paranormal, or they might be the result of a fault in the mechanisms which had activated the appliances.'

It is a curious fact that in many cases of haunting or poltergeist activity, electrical equipment from light switches to fridges, fires and radios seems a popular target. I recently heard of a small electric mower which whirrs away happily unplugged in its cupboard where there is no source of power.

By lucky chance, during a trip to Abbots Langley I visited the antique shop not far from the church. While chatting to Mr Dobson, the owner, I mentioned the reason for my visit and was delighted to find that he actually owned a photograph of Mary Ann Treble, which he kindly allowed me to have copied. It was given to him many years ago by a woman, now dead, who had been a close friend of Mary Ann's, and who had firmly believed that there was a mystery about her death.

In the head and shoulders picture Mary Ann wears a dark dress, buttoned high to the neck, and on her head is perched the kind of small white frilly cap worn by servants in those far-off days. Her hair is parted in the middle and drawn severely back, and her expression is anxious, possibly due to trying to keep perfectly still for the photographer. It is impossible to guess her age when the picture was taken, but she has a pleasant unlined face and hair not yet grey.

Poor Mary Ann. If only she could tell us what happened in that delightful old vicarage that brought her back after death, perhaps to seek redress for her wrongs? Is she at peace yet? Time will tell.

4

The Ghosts of Knebworth

K NEBWORTH House might have been designed as the setting for a film of Gothic romance and horror. Fearsome gargoyles, dragons and strange medieval creatures look down from the turreted battlements of what was once the stately home of the Victorian novelist and politician, Sir Edward Bulwer Lytton.

A keen student of the occult, Bulwer Lytton was responsible for the transformation of his family home from a Tudor mansion which Queen Elizabeth I once came to admire, to the present castellated mansion with its central tower, many cupolas and other strange embellishments. Long after his death, Lytton's eye-catching Gothic fantasy has provided the perfect back-cloth for several films, TV productions and advertisements.

It must have looked a fitting place to welcome the famous medium, Daniel Dunglas Home, when he arrived in England from America in the early summer of 1855. He was perhaps the most extraordinary medium ever known, a man whom royalty, society hostesses and literary lions alike fell over themselves to meet, and one of the first to welcome him into English society was Bulwer Lytton.

Home was invited to Lytton's Park Lane home, and was later a guest at Knebworth where several seances took place. The remarkable phenomena, such as levitating furniture, spirit hands, messages from the dead, and most remarkably, the sight of Home floating through the air provided invaluable material for Lytton, the writer, and

Home's wife resentfully commented that descriptions of supernatural phenomena in Lytton's powerful story, *The Haunters and the Haunted*, read like a transcript of a Home seance.

Did Bulwer Lytton share his family's own ghost stories with Dunglas Home? Like many great families, the Lyttons had their own phantom of doom. Known as the Radiant Boy, or the Yellow Boy, the Lytton ghost traditionally appeared to those destined to die a violent death, when it would mime the manner in which their end would come. Not surprisingly, members of the family could never be induced to spend a night in what was known as The Yellow Boy's Room, but they had no scruples about putting guests in there, after giving them a few hair-raising details of the legendary family spectre.

Many a guest spent a long, terrified night in the haunted room expecting at any moment to be confronted by the Lytton phantom with its unwelcome message. One visitor, an artist named Green, who was allocated the Yellow Boy's Room, afterwards told a friend, the artist W.P. Frith:

'I had seen the infernal room before dinner, and I thought then it looked a ghostly sort of place. When I reached it that night, what would I not have given to be back in my own room at home. I looked under the bed, up the great wide chimney, and had a shock from the sight of my own face in the looking glass. No ghost could be whiter than I was. I don't believe in ghosts you know, but still it was too bad of Lytton to tell me such things just as I was going to bed, and then put me in the very place!

'There was an awful old cabinet in the room. I managed to pull one door open and was tugging at the other when my candle went out – how I don't know – somebody seemed to blow it out. I can't tell you what became of it, all I know is I jumped into bed with my boots on, and lay trembling there for hours, Frith, literally for hours, until sleep took me at last. Never was I more thankful than when I awoke, and saw the sun shining into the Yellow Boy's Room.'

But for one earlier visitor, the night he spent at Knebworth was something more than just a chilling experience.

Lord Castlereagh, then Foreign Secretary, was entertained at Knebworth and inevitably, he was allocated the Yellow Boy's Room to sleep in. Next morning at breakfast, he made no secret of his troubled night.

'I was disturbed in the night in a very startling and unpleasant fashion,' he told his host. 'I was very tired, and was soon asleep. I could not have slept long for the wood fire opposite the foot of my bed was still burning when I started up.

'What awoke me I know not. I looked in the direction of the fire, and saw, sitting with its back towards me, what appeared to be the figure of a boy with long, yellowish hair. As I looked, the figure arose, turned towards me, and drawing back the curtains at the bottom of the bed with one hand, with the other he drew his fingers two or three times across his throat. I saw him as distinctly as I see you now.'

'You must have been dreaming,' replied his host reassuringly. Nevertheless he went on to tell his guest about the family tradition of the ghostly Yellow Boy who only appeared to those destined to die violently, and who indicated by his gestures the manner of their death.

What Lord Castlereagh thought on hearing this disquieting information we do not know. Nor the Lytton family's reactions when some time later, in 1822, the strain of his office proved too much for Lord Castlereagh, and he took his own life by cutting his throat with a penknife.

The Radiant Boy is not the only ghost associated with Knebworth. Around Knebworth hearths on dark winter nights local people used to tell the tale of a young girl imprisoned in a little room in the East Wing to keep her from the man she loved. To pass the time, she spent the long days spinning, but finally maddened by despair, she took her own life. But they would say, if you were to listen by the door of the haunted room you could still hear the whirring of her ghostly spinning wheel.

A privately printed book entitled *The History of Jenny Spinner* purported to tell the truth about Knebworth's phantom spinner, but according to W.B. Gerish, a local historian, it was made up in Christmas 1800 by Elizabeth Maria James, one of the house party who had amused themselves by writing ghost stories.

And yet, an inventory of 1797 did mention 'Spinning Jenny's room', then situated in part of the house later demolished. And one of the gardeners at Knebworth in the middle years of this century said that he had often seen the ghost of Jenny in the kitchen garden.

There have been other incidents of a ghostly nature such as the experience of a recent American guest, sleeping in the four poster bed in the Queen Elizabeth room. She woke early one morning to find a strange girl with long blonde hair leaning over her. Was she the same mysterious female spirit, history unknown, who occasionally haunts the picture gallery?

But according to Lady Cobbold, wife of Bulwer Lytton's great-great grandson, Knebworth is still home to the most appropriate presence of all, Bulwer Lytton himself.

His study, which remains much as he left it, contains his prolific array of published works on the shelves, his favourite pipe and his crystal ball, and a portrait of the great man himself. It has inspired strange uneasy sensations in some visitors, but Lady Cobbold and her son

Henry accept as quite natural that the man who had such a great love for his ancestral home should wish to visit his old haunts, and linger in the rooms which were his for so long.

He is not seen as a ghostly figure, there is simply 'a strong sensation of his presence, both in his study and the adjoining drawing room he used'. The family do not find this frightening at all, but cleaning staff cannot be persuaded to work in these rooms on their own.

What do Knebworth's other-worldly residents make of the pop concerts, jousting, vintage car rallies and other entertainments that bring the crowds to Knebworth these days? There are said to have been reports of burglar alarms going off of their own accord, mysterious shadows and eerie sensations which suggest that Knebworth may be living up to its curiously sinister Gothic exterior.

5

A King's Mistress still lingers . . .

THERE was something oddly disturbing about the tall young man who had appeared so suddenly by the coach house. Perhaps it was his clothes, although the frilly white shirt and dark knee breeches would not have been out of place on a pop singer. There were large shiny buckles on his shoes, and his long fair hair was tied back in a pony tail.

He looked intently at the startled girl, the hint of a smile on his handsome, rather serious young face. But as she looked back at him, feeling uneasy without quite knowing why, she realised that he was beginning to look more and more like a faded photograph. He was disappearing in front of her eyes.

Maria Goldsmith was the girl, and we met in the Tudor cottage where she lived with her husband Robin in the grounds of Salisbury Hall, one of the most haunted houses in the country. The stormy wind outside made the old rafters creak like a ship at sea, but inside it was warm and comfortable with its white walls, oak beams and the soft hiss of a log fire.

Although Maria had lived in the village close by the Hall, she had never heard the ghost stories connected with it, so her meeting with the young Cavalier had the double impact of terror and surprise.

'It was in the summer,' she told me, 'at about half past ten at night. It was still quite light. I remember Robin and I were at the moat, and like a couple of children we started playing hide and seek round the coach house when suddenly I noticed this chap.

'He was very old-fashioned in the way he was dressed, which made me look again. Then as I looked, he seemed to get hazy, and I realised what it must be. I'm afraid I screamed in terror. Robin came rushing down the stairs of the coach house, but he didn't see anything.'

For many years there have been stories about the ghost of a Cavalier being seen in the Hall. Apparently he was carrying secret despatches at the time of the Civil War when he encountered a party of Roundheads, and took refuge in the Hall, with his enemies close behind him. He reached the upper floors, looking desperately for a hiding place but realised too late that there was no escape, and rather than be taken, he killed himself. Some say his ghost has been seen with a sword sticking through him, others that he shot himself.

Robin Goldsmith told me that the passage where the ghost walks used to run right through the house into the Tudor wing, now demolished. Many people, including Robin's mother, had heard footsteps at night passing along the passage when no one else was there.

Lady Gresley, wife of Sir Nigel Gresley, designer of the record-breaking Pacific steam locomotives, lived at the Hall in the thirties and had the terrifying experience of actually seeing the Cavalier's ghost enter her bedroom one night. She was so frightened that she never slept in that room again. Was this the young Cavalier that Maria encountered? It seems likely that this may have been a different manifestation.

At the time of Maria's ghostly visitation Robin's family lived in Salisbury Hall, a lovely mellow old house near London Colney, with a long history and many memorable owners over the centuries. A narrow lane turning off from the B556 road between London and St Albans leads to an ancient medieval bridge, fording the moat which surrounds this peaceful oasis, set in rolling farmland with a distant view of St Albans Abbey.

When the Goldsmith family made Salisbury Hall their home it was almost derelict and overgrown with brambles, and it was a labour of love to restore and furnish it. They found that gardening was something of an archeological treasure hunt as relics of earlier times came to light, and a growing collection of old coins, buckles, spurs, broken remnants of swords and ancient tiles told their own story of a past which seems very close there.

The Domesday Book records a Saxon manor on the site, and at the time of the Wars of the Roses, the great Warwick the Kingmaker, resplendent in his Lancastrian armour, rode out in 1471 from the manor, then simply called Salisbury's, to defeat and death in the Battle of Barnet. Later, Henry VIII's treasurer built himself a fine mansion there, of which little remains.

But perhaps Salisbury Hall's most interesting memories belong to the time when it was the setting for one of the most romantic liaisons of history. The hall was bought secretly on behalf of Charles II the year his love affair with Nell Gwynn began, and extensive improvements and alterations were soon under way to turn the house into a royal hideaway, far from the intrigues and prying eyes of the Court, where the Merry Monarch could snatch a little summer love with his beloved Nell.

The flint and brick building beside the moat has always been known as Nell Gwynn's cottage, and when Robin and Maria got married they decided to make their home there.

It is believed that Nell Gwynn's first son was born at Salisbury Hall, and was looked after by nurses in the cottage. Maria and I opened the little diamond paned window in the cottage bedroom and looked down to the moat below.

'This is where Nell Gwynn is supposed to have held her baby out of the window and threatened to throw him into the moat if Charles didn't give him a title,' said Maria. 'Charles, perhaps inspired by the sight of St Albans Abbey across the fields, said "Pray spare the Duke of St Albans".'

Nell Gwynn is Salisbury Hall's most famous ghost, and there have been sightings of King Charles's pretty mistress in one of the bedrooms and in the panelled Crown Chamber downstairs.

Winston Churchill's beautiful mother Jenny once lived at Salisbury Hall with her second husband, George Cornwallis-West. In those days, the cream of Edwardian society danced in the ballroom, now vanished, and the singer Dame Nellie Melba, the great actress Eleanora Duse, and Edward VII were also among the visitors. In fact, Winston found his lively mother's social whirl too much at times, and would escape to his tree house in a tall lime tree at the back of the house where he could retreat to read and write his speeches in peace.

George Cornwallis-West once saw an unknown young woman standing at the foot of the stairs. She looked at him intently, then turned and went through the door into a passage, and puzzled, he followed, but she had disappeared. Although sceptical about ghosts until then, he realised that this was no ordinary visitor. In fact, her resemblance to a maid at his mother's home made him feel afraid that something might have happened to the girl.

However, enquiries reassured him. Everything was fine, in fact the maid was just on the point of getting married! It was sometime later, when looking at a picture of Nell Gwynn that he noticed the striking resemblance between Nell and his mother's maid, and realised who the mysterious lady must have been.

I asked Robin Goldsmith if he had had any supernatural

experiences at Salisbury Hall. He laughed, and said, 'I slept in the little room over the porch for seven years, and I didn't see or hear a thing.'

This room had an eerie reputation for many years. 'I used to stay in the house sometimes when Robin and I were engaged,' remarked Maria, 'and one night I slept in the room over the porch as there was no other room available.

'I had a terrible feeling when I first went in. I hadn't heard anything about the room being haunted, I just felt I wanted to get away, and went to bed feeling quite miserable. There was a clock in there that chimed every hour, so Robin stopped it in case it woke me up.

'Well, I did wake up! It was about 2 am and the first thing I noticed was that the clock was ticking away merrily again. Then the bed began to rock quite violently back and forth for about three minutes.

'You can imagine,' she continued with a reminiscent shudder, 'how I huddled under the bedclothes, absolutely paralysed with fear. I thought I must be dreaming. I got up next morning at about six. I couldn't wait to get out of there, but I didn't say a word to anybody. I thought they'd think I was mad.

'But in the end I told Robin's mother what had happened, and she showed me a book which says that about the time of the First World War, a governess slept there, and that "something terrifying" came out of the wall in the night, and approached her bed. Apparently she was too scared to sleep in the house again.'

When I had visited Salisbury Hall previously, I thought that one part of the garden had a particularly serene and happy atmosphere. I mentioned this to Maria. 'Yes,' she said, 'that is where they hear the laughter.'

Apparently at times people have heard the echoes of a lovely rich laugh floating across the garden. Is it Nell

Gwynn? Somehow the past seems very close at Salisbury Hall, and I feel sure Nell was happy here once long ago . . . and perhaps she still comes back sometimes.

Note: Unfortunately Salisbury Hall is no longer open to the public as it is now occupied as business premises. Access is still available to the Mosquito Aircraft Museum in the grounds. The hall was a secret aircraft design centre in the Second World War where the first Mosquito was designed and built in 1940.

6

The Wicked Lady of Markyate

LATE one winter night in December 1970, Douglas Payne, manager of the Wicked Lady pub, was giving his dog a last run on Nomansland Common before bed, as he often did. He was surprised when suddenly he heard the sound of a horse galloping fast in his direction. It was coming nearer and nearer until it passed so close that he felt he could almost have touched it. But, chillingly, there was absolutely nothing to see. Mr Payne knew he hadn't imagined it, and the terrified reaction of his dog showed that he too had shared this strange, uncanny experience.

The inn sign swinging outside his pub close by showed the mocking masked face of a beautiful highwaywoman. And Mr Payne was not slow to realise that he had probably just had an uncomfortably close encounter with the real thing! That is, if you can call a ghost nearly 300 years old 'real'. But for many people in the Hertfordshire village of Markyate and its neighbourhood, ghosts don't come much more real than Lady Katherine Ferrers, known as the Wicked Lady.

The story of Katherine Ferrers is as romantic as fiction. She was born at the home of the Ferrers family, Markyate Cell, a Tudor mansion built by Humphrey Bourchier on the site of the 12th century Priory of St Trinity-in-the-Wood. It had been the home of the Ferrers family for generations when Sir Knighton Ferrers married his beautiful bride, the heiress Lady Katherine Walters. Sadly, Sir Knighton died in 1640, leaving his wife with a six year old daughter, also called Katherine, who was his heiress as two sons had died the previous year.

It was a time when the country was in the grip of the Civil War, and many of the King's supporters were desperate for money. A rich young widow was unlikely to be alone for long and Lady Katherine was soon remarried to Sir Simon Fanshawe of Ware Park, a strong Royalist.

When Parliamentary forces overran Ware Park, and her husband was on the run from Cromwell's men, Lady Katherine and her little daughter took refuge with Lady Bedell in Huntingdonshire. They were there until young Katherine reached the age of twelve, then the legal age to marry, when Sir Simon immediately married her to his 16 year old son Thomas, to get his hands on her fortune.

It seems unlikely that the young couple ever lived together. The youthful bride stayed with her mother and Lady Bedell, and her groom returned to the family's estate in Ireland.

Poor Katherine found herself almost entirely alone a few years later when both her mother and Lady Bedell died and, neglected by her husband's family, she returned, lonely and disillusioned, to live in her childhood home, Markyate Cell. It must have been an empty existence for a young and beautiful girl, and just what inspired her to turn to a reckless life of crime can only be imagined. At that time it was not unusual for the younger sons of good families to try highway robbery as a temporary means of livelihood, but an old account says that Katherine 'took to highway robbery for the sheer love of adventure and the exercise of manly attributes'.

In her beautiful house a concealed staircase led to a small secret room, built into the kitchen chimney. Here Katherine kept her highwayman disguise, and at night the lady of the manor would change into buckskin breeches, riding cloak, three-cornered hat, and the vital mask. Riding a black horse, she held up and robbed the long distance coaches travelling through the rutted Hertfordshire lanes. As a much feared mystery highwayman, she had the reputation of mercilessly shooting down any traveller who showed resistance to her demands.

Just when she met Ralph Chaplin, a farmer turned highwayman is not known. Some say it was he who introduced her to the dangerous life she found such an adventure. In the Margaret Lockwood film *The Wicked Lady* her lover and partner in crime played by James Mason is probably a glamorised version of Ralph Chaplin. And no doubt the real Chaplin seemed a dashing enough character to the young and impressionable Katherine. But Chaplin eventually met the fate that awaited many a gentleman of the road, and during a hold-up his luck ran out and he was shot dead on Finchley Common.

Savage in her grief, Katherine is said to have become more violent, adding arson and murder to her crimes. The parish constable at nearby Caddington was shot dead on his doorstep when he answered a call one night, houses in the area were set on fire, farm animals were found slaughtered, and travellers along Watling Street after dark knew that they took their lives in their hands.

Katherine Ferrers was still in her mid-twenties when she held up her last victim on Nomansland Common. A waggon was passing through the Common on the way to Gustard Wood just as night was falling, when the figure of a highwayman suddenly leapt out of the trees in front of it. Without hesitation Katherine shot the driver, unaware that he had given a lift to two other men who were in the back of the cart among the bales. One of them fired back at Katherine, badly wounding her, and she fled, riding full speed for the haven of her hidden room. But her wound was a fatal one, and she collapsed and died outside the entrance to her secret stairway, where her body was found. Her highwayman gear and the black horse running loose in the grounds identified her as the mysterious highwayman who had terrorised the area. An entry in Ware Parish Register records that Katherine Fanshawe, wife of Thomas Fanshawe of Ware Park, was buried on 13th June 1660. Her body is believed to have been taken to St Mary's church at Ware secretly at night, but she was not interred in the Fanshawe family vault. The doorway to her secret chamber in Markyate Cell was bricked up and for more than a hundred years no one attempted to enter Lady Ferrers' hideaway.

But she was not forgotten. From the day of her death, the stories of her robberies and her secret double life circulated round the village. Some said she had buried her ill-gotten wealth somewhere in the grounds, and repeated this little rhyme:

Near the Cell there is a well,
Near the well there is a tree,
And 'neath the tree the treasure be.

But to date, no one seems to have unearthed her valuable haul.

Markyate soon realised that they had not heard the last of their Wicked Lady. First one, then another reported seeing her ghost in highwayman garb riding hell for leather on horseback, or even swinging high in the branches of some of the old trees near her home.

In 1840, part of the house was destroyed by fire, blamed by villagers on Katherine Ferrers, and some of the local men who helped to put out the blaze insisted that they distinctly saw her ghost watching them. During the rebuilding work which followed, the owner decided to re-open the doorway to Katherine's secret room, but none of the locals would undertake the work. Workmen had to be brought down from London in the end, and there were reports of sighs and groans being heard for which there was no obvious explanation.

When the doorway was unblocked, a narrow stone staircase was found with a heavy oak door at the top. The workmen broke this down but found afterwards that a concealed spring would have opened it easily. The room itself was disappointing, containing nothing but cobwebs and a few bats.

Augustus Hare (1834 – 1903) reported in his Journal for November 1894 that Katherine Ferrers constantly haunted Markyate Cell: 'Mr Adey, who lives there now, meets her on the stairs and wishes her Goodnight. Once seeing her with arms outstretched in a doorway, he called to his wife who was outside "Now we've got her", and then they rushed upon her from both sides, but caught nothing.'

The ghost made a startling appearance once at a parish tea party in the grounds, and many locals claimed to have seen her around Markyate. A Mr George Wood who celebrated his diamond wedding in 1969 told the local paper of an evening more than 60 years before when he was walking down the road to Kensworth after visiting his wife-to-be in Markyate:

'It was a clear moonlight night when I saw the ghost clearly,' he said. 'She was about half a mile away. I noticed the clothes she was wearing and saw her disappear into a ditch at the side of the road.' When he reached the place where the figure had been, there was no trace.

'I was told later by a woman in Markyate that the ghost of the Wicked Lady walked regularly, and that was what I had seen', he said.

In 1912, council workmen were extending the sewer system from the High Street at Markyate to Hicks Lane, now Hicks Road, reputed to be one of Katherine Ferrers' haunts. The night watchman set out the warning lamps to indicate the road works, kindled a fire in his brazier and made himself cosy in his hut for the night. After a while he noticed someone staring down into the trench outside, and called out but got no reply.

Later he described his visitor to the local press: 'He was a young man, slight in build, with long dark hair dangling about his shoulders. He wore long leather boots which seemed to extend to his thigh, as far as I could see, but a dark knee-length cloak which appeared to have several ornate clasps obscured the lower part of his body.'

The watchman challenged the figure again, and when there was still no response he began to feel alarmed and ran down to the High Street to seek assistance. He knocked up the village policeman, who came back with the watchman to search round the site, but there was no one about and they found nothing.

Markyate's bypass was made in 1957, and a similar incident was reported then when the Irish watchman sitting by his fire one night looked up to see someone warming their hands by the brazier. He thought it was a young man, but when the figure suddenly disappeared, he was convinced that what he had seen was Markyate's legendary phantom.

Does Hertfordshire's Wicked Lady still ride the lanes round Markyate, Nomansland and thereabouts? Perhaps one moonlight night you may hear the sound of galloping hooves as a sudden chill wind rushes by leaving you wondering and afraid. Will Hertfordshire ever really see the last of the wicked Lady Katherine Ferrers?

7

The Ghostly Monk
of Ayot St Lawrence

A YOT St Lawrence is a small but very interesting village with picturesque cottages and a Queen Anne manor house, its gateposts adorned by curious heraldic cats, each holding a hand, the insignia of ancestors of Lord Brocket.

The old church is a romantic ruin, partially demolished by Sir Lyonel Lyde, the then Lord of the Manor, who decided it was spoiling the view from his house. The Bishop of Lincoln put a stop to the demolition as soon as he heard what Sir Lyonel was doing, but by then it was badly damaged and open to the sky, and as it would have cost £1,256.8s.10d to restore the church to its former state, it soon became an ivy clad ruin.

Sir Lyonel thought that something resembling a Greek temple would be more to his taste, and in 1779 he built new St Lawrence, designed by Nicholas Revett, who was inspired by the antiquities he had admired in Athens.

Ayot St Lawrence was the home of George Bernard Shaw, and Shaw's Corner where he lived from 1906 to 1950 is now National Trust property, open to the public. His library, the summer house where he worked, and many of his personal possessions are as he left them.

The village is steeped in history, and its ancient inn, the Brocket Arms, with its splendid heraldic sign swinging in the breeze, looks the perfect location for mysterious tales of the supernatural. Inside there are old oak beams and inglenook fireplaces with welcoming log fires blazing in the hearth in wintertime and yet, despite its old world charm, the Brocket Arms has long had the reputation of being haunted.

Some years ago I visited the inn to meet Mrs Teresa Sweeney who had worked there as a part-time barmaid for many years. I was curious to hear at first hand her account of her meeting with the pub's resident spirit.

'I was just coming in with some sandwiches one day,' she told me, 'when I noticed someone standing in the corner of the room. I thought "Goodness, who's that?" then I realised it was a monk! He was a little man, dressed all in brown in a monk's habit. His head was bent so I couldn't see his face because of his cowl, but as I stood staring at him, he just vanished.'

Although her encounter with the phantom monk was quite a shock, Teresa was not entirely surprised. Like the landlord's family, she had often heard footsteps and other noises for which there seemed to be no natural explanation. But Teresa believed she was the first person to actually see the old inn's spectral regular. Then a few months later, she was to have another unnerving glimpse of the ghostly monk of the Brocket Arms.

She was busy in the dining room one morning when, looking up, she was startled to see a face staring at her through the glass-topped door leading to the bar. She described it as a thin, old face, rather hazy, and the monkish garb he was wearing convinced her that it was the same strange apparition she had seen before. And once again, as she looked at him, he faded away before her eyes.

Mrs Sweeney told me that they often heard sounds overhead such as footsteps, bangs and thumps when they knew there was no one up there. 'The landlord's wife has heard a lot of banging about upstairs, but she hasn't seen a ghost.'

When I asked Mrs Sweeney if she thought that there was more than one ghost at the inn she replied: 'Sometimes there have been sounds like a lot of men's voices talking together. You see, it used to be a place where monks could stay, a hostelry for pilgrims.'

One night as she came downstairs she was terrified to hear the sound of little tapping feet following her down, step by step. 'I thought, oh, not again. I just galloped down into the bar, and banged the door shut behind me.'

When a place is as old as the Brocket Arms, there are bound to be all kinds of stories. Part of the building dates back to 1378, when it was built as a monks' hostel, and rumour has it that there is supposed to be a secret passage running under the roadway to the ruined church opposite.

So why does the ghost of a monk linger in the Brocket Arms? Tradition has it that a monk once hanged himself in what is now the bar, but the rest of the story is lost in the mists of time. However, it appears as if one unfortunate pilgrim had an interrupted journey, and decided to stay.

8

The Grey Lady
of Bishops Stortford

BISHOPS Stortford is a charming old town on the borders of Hertfordshire and Essex, many of its buildings little changed in appearance since medieval times. It takes its name from the river Stort which runs by the remains of Waytemore Castle, a fortress with a dark history built by William the Conqueror, who gave the deeds of the manor to the Bishop of London and his successors. Cecil Rhodes was born and educated here, and his birthplace is now a museum.

A place like this, full of history, is likely to have many tales of supernatural happenings, but most of them are attributed to one active and ubiquitous apparition, Bishops Stortford's famous ghost, the Grey Lady.

There is an ancient house in Bridge Street which was once the country home of successive Bishops of London, and a bridge used to run across the road to what is now the Black Lion inn. This picturesque timbered building is believed to have been the servants' quarters, and both this and the old Boars Head have had sightings of the mysterious Grey Lady. Rumour has it that she once passed through a bar full of customers in broad daylight, and out of the door, but there are few details of this remarkable event.

Passages or a tunnel led from the old Bishops' house to Waytemore Castle, used in the 16th century as a prison by the much feared Bishop Bonner, notorious for his persecution of Protestant reformers. There is little doubt that the deep, dark dungeons there saw the last hours of many wretched prisoners, and some years ago in a triangular piece of ground near the castle mound the remains of a charred stake were discovered, at which a man had been burnt.

The history of Bishops Stortford recalls a similar event. One of Bonner's victims died in the flames because he would not renounce his faith, and his fellow prisoner, due to die in a like manner at Saffron Walden, was cruelly forced to watch the martyrdom of his friend. It would be hardly surprising if such scenes of anguish had left a heritage of haunting, but does not explain the mysterious identity of the ghostly Grey Lady.

Eventually the Bishops' house was incorporated in a department store called Handscombs, and this building for many years has been the focus of paranormal happenings attributed to the Grey Lady. Some of the activity has been of a violent poltergeist nature, with many articles being thrown about and loud knockings and other unexplained noises.

Mr J. Lowe, who used to own the shop some years ago, was working late one night until about 1 am. As he went down the stairs, 'I saw the figure of a lady dressed in grey in front of me. She turned to the left and then went up the back stairs. She simply came from nowhere, and I did not see her face.

'Another time we were working late and I distinctly heard someone coming up the stairs. The footsteps came right to the door and I called out "Come in", but of course, there was no one there.'

Mr Lowe said that during his occupation of the shop some human bones were discovered underneath an old cupboard. When afterwards these were decently buried he thought that there would be an end to the haunting, but it does not seem to have been the case.

When the shop was taken over by the Maslen Group, on one occasion when Mr L.G. Maslen was working in the office he heard something rush along the passage outside, reputedly haunted by the Grey Lady. He told himself it was probably a cat, but he really thought it sounded much more like a person.

On another occasion two of his employees were working upstairs one night when they heard a crash and the sound of running feet. They each took a different staircase and hurried downstairs, but found nothing to account for the noise.

When Mr Maslen's son Peter was a schoolboy, he and his friends spent weekends excavating what was thought to be a tunnel leading to the castle, but they gave up after hearing strange noises from time to time.

During alterations to the shop some years ago, the workmen who were often there at night or at weekends when the shop was closed were alarmed by what they described as a 'terrifying presence'. One Sunday they suddenly noticed curious swishing sounds behind them, and when they looked round they found freshly made slashes in the plaster they had just finished, which looked as if it had been clawed with great force.

In an attempt to find a reason for the strange happenings at the shop, the Maslen Group invited a two-man team from Cambridge University to investigate, and they were of the opinion that the premises were definitely haunted by two ghosts. They thought that one was a man who was quite harmless, but the other was a woman of a very violent nature.

Certainly this tallies with the way articles have been thrown around, sometimes apparently aimed at people, and on one occasion a large dinner service suddenly slid off a shelf when no human presence was close by, and the whole lot crashed to the floor.

While researching this book I talked to two of the assistants now working at this much haunted store, and was shown a display of kitchen knives which they say sometimes jump off the wall of their own accord. And from time to time some rolls of lace curtaining on a stand suddenly unroll noisily, though no one is near them.

Opposite the top of Bridge Street stands the handsome old coaching inn, The George, dating from 1417, and this too is on the wandering Grey Lady's visiting list. The focus of the haunting is Room 27 which has the chilling reputation that something not of this world is lurking within its walls, and this particular room and the passage outside are said to be no place for people of a nervous disposition.

A couple of overnight guests were badly frightened, and a workman who knew nothing about the ghost was so scared by the atmosphere he sensed around him that he abandoned his work and fled.

Some visitors have refused to consider spending the night there after experiencing a dreadful feeling that a terrifying invisible 'something' was watching them, and others have left in alarm after seeing doors and wardrobes open without human intervention. The staff too, have seen a 'white shape' hovering in the cellar.

A grey figure has also appeared in a dark passage leading to the storeroom of a shop nearby. It was described as a tall mass which moved fairly quickly into the storeroom and then disappeared through the back wall.

Yet another port of call on the Grey Lady's rounds is the shop owned by Tissiman and Sons in the High Street, where she has been seen several times. This is a Tudor building that was previously the Old House Café, and a lady who worked there during World War Two as a waitress said that the ghost appeared there regularly. She believed there used to be old passages underground linking the building to The George nearby.

Two daughters of her employer told her they were woken up in the mornings by the sound of children laughing and rolling marbles along the floor. One of the girls saw the Grey Lady standing at the foot of the stairs one day, and at the time she distinctly smelt burning wood when there were no fires in use.

So who is Bishops Stortford's very active Grey Lady, if indeed only one ghost is responsible for such a busy schedule of haunting? In a town with such a long and interesting history there must be a wide choice of candidates. The smell of burning wood when she appeared at the Old House Café prompts a rather macabre thought. Could she have been one of Bishop Bonner's victims burnt at the stake?

One haunted pub outside the Grey Lady's orbit is the 16th century Cock Inn, a place where grooms and their horses used to put up on what was the London to Cambridge route. Legend has it that pretty, witty Nell Gwynn once stayed there while her lover, King Charles II was accommodated in grander surroundings at The George.

The Cock's two ghosts are a gentleman in Civil War garb and a serving wench, and the landlord's wife, Mrs Molly Tunks, has seen them several times. 'They just appear and disappear very quickly so you have to stop and think if you have seen them at all,' she told a local newspaper in 1988.

She says she likes having them around and doesn't find their presence frightening. But a few years ago major renovations to the pub had psychic repercussions. Tables flew across rooms and lamps were smashed, and there was a feeling of unnatural cold in the building, which spoiled its usual cosy atmosphere. When someone suggested that the ghosts might be upset at the alterations taking place,

Mrs Tunks put flowers everywhere to make the old inn feel more like home, and she reassured the ghosts that the work was going to make a big improvement. And after that the pub returned to normal, ghosts and all!

9

Ghosts
of the Wayside

IN the realms of ghost lore there is a category of
itinerant phantom one could describe as road or wayside
ghosts. These are the shadowy forms sometimes half-
glimpsed by the side of the road as one drives by late on
a dark night.

Perhaps you pause, looking back, wondering whether
to offer a lift to the solitary pedestrian who obviously has
a long way to go on this lonely road. But if you draw up,
or glance back, the road is empty. Puzzled and perhaps
a little disturbed you drive on.

If this has happened to you, you may have encountered
one of the many spectral jay-walkers that pursue their
mysterious journey along Britain's country roads. Where
do they come from, and where do they go? Some seem
as nebulous as mist, or a shadow, others are more
alarming and potentially dangerous. These are the ghostly
figures which unexpectedly rush across the road, usually
at night, just as a motorist is approaching. Sometimes
there is a bump, and the shocked driver pulls up,
convinced that he has run into some reckless pedestrian
who practically flung himself beneath the wheels. The
story is always the same. When the driver gets out, there
is no body lying there in the road, and no sign of damage
to the car.

The driver, bemused and frightened by his eerie
experience, drives on, trying to find some rational
explanation for what seemed an all too genuine happening

at the time. Did it in fact really happen, or was it some kind of hallucination created by the lateness of the hour, shadows on a deserted road, and a tired driver startled by the swift darting of an animal or bird in front of him? Sometimes this may be so, but undeniably there are places with a history of such happenings that are perhaps best avoided by the nervous traveller.

Britain's highways and byways are crowded and busy places, and yet phantom stage coaches still arrive at wayside inns, horses and riders, often strangely headless, gallop through woodlands and lanes, spectral carts pass noiselessly by, and ghostly buses or lorries can be an unsuspected hazard on the streets.

Mardleybury Manor at Woolmer Green, mentioned in the Domesday Book, has a history of haunting, inside and out. In April 1968 a Mr Newton who lived nearby was driving home when as he passed the manor, the figure of a woman in old-fashioned grey clothing suddenly dashed in front of his car. It was impossible to avoid her; he felt the impact and skidded to a standstill. Badly shaken he got out of the car, but was mystified, and no doubt relieved, to find no sign of the woman he appeared to have collided with.

In 1980 another motorist, driving near the bottom of Whitehorse Lane approaching Woolmer Green, suddenly saw a figure with long hair and a flowing gown or cape right in front of him. It seemed impossible to miss her, and he veered off the road hitting a tree. But although he feared he had run into the pedestrian, when he looked round there was no one there. Other drivers passing the manor who have reported similar experiences, say that the woman's figure is so clear that they have braked hard in an attempt to avoid her.

The story is that many years ago there was a party at Mardleybury Manor and, as one young lady was leaving in her carriage, the driver lost control and the carriage overturned into the pond opposite, drowning the passenger.

A similar but more sinister ghost story concerns the village of Much Hadham where the Bishops of London once had their palace. There, every 13th February, a phantom is said to appear from the ditch at Moat Farm below Kettle Green, attempting to lure passers-by into the moat where her body was thrown after she had been murdered.

At Willian Road, Letchworth Gate, yet another shadowy jay-walker was reported in the *Herts and Beds Citizen* in January 1970. A motorist saw a woman with black hair and a grey coat cross right in front of his vehicle.

'She never faltered,' he said, 'and I had to brake to avoid hitting her. Then she disappeared.'

Just beyond Markyate on the busy road to Dunstable stands the Packhorse Inn. In May 1970 it was reported in the *Luton Evening Post* that two taxi drivers had separately told how they had seen the apparition of a tall man in cricket gear, who suddenly emerged from the shadows into the road in front of them, and then vanished. This is not the first time the ghost has been seen by passing motorists, and it is thought to be the apparition of a cricketer who was killed in an accident at this spot in the 1950s.

Most motorists would, of course, stop if held up by a policeman, and a couple driving along Holy Cross Hill, Hoddesdon in the 1960s, drew up when their headlights revealed the figure of a police constable standing in the middle of the road. They wound down the window to ask him what was the matter, and just had time to notice that the man was wearing strangely old-fashioned uniform before he vanished in front of their eyes. This is said to be only one of several similar sightings of the same figure on Holy Cross Hill.

Whitehorse Lane which lies on the boundary between Datchworth and Welwyn takes its name from the ghost of a headless white horse sometimes heard galloping down the lane from Burnham Green, where the sign of the White Horse pub commemorates a tragic happening at the time of the Civil War. Cromwell's men caught and beheaded one of King Charles's supporters at his farm in the area, but when they tried to take his white horse away with them the fine creature resisted so strongly that they beheaded him too.

Locals say that animals are reluctant to pass that way at night.

Not far away Hawkins Hall Lane, Datchworth, is haunted by the figure of a little old lady in a black dress, seen shuffling along the road. Those who have seen her say that from the back she appears to be bent with age, but seen from the front it is alarmingly clear that she has no head. It is believed she may be an old woman who was so unhappy after the death of her husband that she hanged herself in her cottage nearby.

She is not Datchworth's only ghost. In 1769, a destitute family were taken to the local poorhouse where they all died soon afterwards. According to local history, their bodies were taken on a cart to the graveyard for a paupers' burial, and in a ghostly re-enactment of the scene, a phantom cart has been seen passing along Rectory Lane, Datchworth, with legs dangling pathetically from the back of the cart. And oddly enough, no horse is visible.

But there are many stories of meetings with spectral horses and riders, coaches and even Boadicea's chariot in Pendley Beeches, near Tring. People walking or driving past there late at night have sometimes encountered a ghostly rider coming down the pathway from Wigginton and, one New Years Eve, a four-in-hand coach with a headless coachman and horses was seen in the same area.

Another type of transport sometimes seen on the 1st May has been Boadicea's chariot, and to see this coming up Pendley Beeches was considered an ill omen.

One old wayside inn apparently has customers who continue to call centuries later. A letter in *Hertfordshire Countryside* magazine in May 1984 told how someone travelling on the Elstree to Radlett road during the previous winter had on no less than three occasions seen a coach and horses standing opposite the Waggon and Horses public house. On each occasion a man dressed in jacket, knee breeches and three-cornered hat helped a lady in grey down from the coach. Then they crossed the road and disappeared into the inn.

But older ghosts than these still stalk Hertfordshire. The Romans were here for centuries, and some of them still are, if various sightings are to be believed.

A local resident was returning from Wheathampstead to St Albans by car not long ago. It was a cold misty November night, and she was surprised to hear the sound of tramping feet, and a metallic jingling noise. To her amazement, the car's headlights picked out a marching column of Roman legionaries, a standard bearer with a banner at their head. The others with her in the car heard the sounds, but saw nothing.

A friend who lived in Hitchin once told me about the night he took his dog for a late run in the Priory grounds before bedtime. He sat down on the grass, smoking his pipe while the dog ran about, and suddenly he heard the tramp of marching feet, and the sound of men's voices talking. He turned, and saw a troop of Roman soldiers approaching, the moonlight glinting on their armour, and as he watched in amazement, they marched past him and on into the mists of time.

The Bucks Advertiser for July 1835 reported that on several successive days at around 6 am a group of Roman soldiers had been seen on Wigginton Common, near Tring, and commented 'Some onlookers were observed to walk through them!'

And the inhabitants of Berkhamsted blame Oliver Cromwell for the destruction of Berkhamsted Castle. They say that sometimes just as daylight is fading, in the lane called Soldiers Bottom, you may encounter a party of Cromwell's Roundheads, the setting sun gleaming on their helmets and armour.

But what of wayside ghosts who come too close for comfort? On the fringe of Hertfordshire we have an example of that modern spectre of the highways and byways, the phantom hitch-hiker.

In 1979 a young man called Roy Fulton was driving home from a darts match in Leighton Buzzard in his Mini van. As he passed along Peddars Lane, Stanbridge, he saw a man standing by the roadside ahead, thumbing a lift.

He drew up a little way in front of the hitch-hiker, and in his van's headlights saw that it was a young man in a dark sweater, open-necked white shirt and dark trousers. The man walked towards Roy's van, opened the door and sat down in the passenger seat without speaking. Roy asked where he wanted to go and, without answering, the man pointed ahead, which Roy assumed meant Dunstable or Totternhoe. He drove on and, after a few minutes, to be friendly Roy turned to offer his silent passenger a cigarette. And found himself alone!

Totally at a loss, Roy braked and looked into the back of the van, and back along the road behind, but the hitch-hiker was nowhere to be seen. The car door had not opened, or he would have noticed the light come on, and in any case the passenger could hardly have alighted from a moving vehicle.

Shaken by his uncanny experience, Roy Fulton drove to the nearest pub for a much needed drink and was, not surprisingly, greeted with the words 'You look as if you've seen a ghost!' Which by now he thought he probably had! Afterwards he reported his experience to Dunstable police, who checked the area but found nothing.

This happening joins a long list of many such encounters with phantom hitch-hikers throughout the world. Some appear to have a connection with a previous fatal accident at the spot where the ghost has been seen, although this did not appear to be the case in the Roy Fulton incident.

Do phantom hitch-hikers and midnight jay-walkers from past centuries represent a genuine experience of the paranormal or are they some kind of hallucination? Whatever the truth of the matter, there is little doubt that to those concerned they have an alarming reality.

10

Little Boy Lost (Part 1)

A NEW shopping precinct may not seem the most likely place to encounter ghosts, but if you visit Christopher Place, St Albans it is just possible that someone who lived around there about 200 years ago may be closer than you might like to imagine.

Some of today's shoppers entering Christopher Place from the Market Place entrance may remember the old Wellington pub which stood on the right for more than 150 years. The exterior of the upper part of the building is unchanged, its ground floor now replaced by shops, but the entrance where coaches once drove in over the cobblestones to the inn yard and the stables at the back are now just a memory. A memory that includes a tragedy, for it is believed that once a child living at the inn ran out as a coach turned into the yard and died beneath the wheels.

But that was in the days of the old Blue Boar which was there before the Wellington, way back in the 17th century, and on into the first half of the 19th century when the innkeeper was Samuel Wildbore, who kept a tame boar as a pet.

No one today remembers the Blue Boar, except of course for the ghost who seems to have lingered in the home he once knew through all the many changes as if, as far as he is concerned, they had never happened.

Do ghosts take account of the alterations that time brings to their old familiar haunts? Rebuilding and modernisation are notorious for stirring old spirits into fresh activity. But where a wing has been pulled down, a floor level changed, or an old doorway bricked up, this apparently means little to any resident spirit who persistently follows his or her familiar haunts above or below existing floors and into areas long since demolished.

Some years ago I visited the Wellington pub in St Albans Market Place to discover if there was any truth in the rumours that it was haunted.

'I used to be sceptical about these things, but so many things have happened I feel sure there's something here,' the new landlord, Frank Jupp, told me. He looked worried. He and his wife and two small children had recently moved in and it was unwelcome news to hear that their new home was reputed to have a ghost. They frankly admitted they would have thought twice about it if they had known.

I looked round the cosy bar decorated with interesting old prints, maps and military souvenirs of the days of the Iron Duke. It was difficult to imagine that on several occasions during the past year it had been the scene of a seance, when members of a psychical research group had tried to contact the supernatural presence responsible for the sequence of happenings at the Wellington which seemed to defy natural explanation.

Even as we talked, there was a noise as if someone was moving furniture about in the living quarters overhead. Mr Jupp went up to investigate, and came back saying both his small children were fast asleep, and everything was as usual up there.

'Must have been the dog,' we said. And then we noticed that the Jupp's friendly old dog was dozing peacefully behind the bar.

The previous landlords, Mr and Mrs Harry Tew, had stayed a year, and from the start they experienced some odd incidents. The cellar door would slowly open by itself, and shut with a crash. There would be the sound of heavy footsteps overhead or furniture being moved about when everyone was downstairs, but when a search was made, there was never anyone there, and nothing had been disturbed. The landlord and his wife were level-headed people, who tried to find reasonable explanations for what was happening.

But before long their young son became nervous about going to bed, insisting that someone he couldn't see came into his room at night and bounced up and down on the end of his bed. His parents, who until then had been sceptical about such things as ghosts, began to think they might have taken on something besides a rather creaky old building.

But Sylvia Bacon, the barmaid, was not surprised. She had worked at the Wellington for years, and it was not her first experience of the old pub's playful and mischievous ghost. When her own children were small, playing hide and seek upstairs with a former landlord's child, they had hidden in a wardrobe. Hearing the bedroom door open, and footsteps approaching their hiding place, they sprang out to surprise their playmate, only to find there was no one there.

Sylvia told me that a visitor staying at the pub had been woken in the night by a rustling sound which seemed to be coming from the wardrobe, so he switched on the light over his bed and looked round. The room was empty, but he found that all his clothes had been pulled off the hangers and thrown out on to the floor.

A succession of landlords over the years were soon made aware of the Wellington's unseen resident who busily moved things from one place to another, opened the cellar door and let it go with a bang, turned the lights on and off and flushed the loo. Sometimes customers' coats would disappear, and be found neatly folded somewhere else, and once a bag of golf clubs propped up behind a door suddenly shot forward and somersaulted into the middle of the bar floor.

Who or whatever it was appeared to have quite a mischievous sense of humour, and once when a sceptical customer confidently declared there were no such things as ghosts, a soda syphon rose slowly in the air and gently settled down again in front of him!

More annoyingly, sometimes the beer gave out unexpectedly and, when the landlord went to investigate, he found that the supply of gas which forced the beer out of the pump had been mysteriously turned off in the cellar.

But it was Sylvia, the barmaid, who was the focus of many of the unaccountable happenings. One morning before opening time she put clean ash-trays on each table, then pushed a pile of crisp packets out of the way while she wiped down the bar.

'When I turned round,' she told me, 'I just went cold. A packet of crisps had been placed in each ash-tray.'

On another occasion she was in the cellar tapping a new barrel of beer before opening time when she heard a loud impatient rapping from the bar. Sylvia was puzzled as she thought the outer doors were still closed, but called out 'I won't be a minute'.

But the brisk tattoo went on and on, and she shot up the cellar steps ready to give the urgent customer a piece of her mind. The bar was empty, the outer doors still locked, and there was no one else around.

There were times when Sylvia had the chilling sensation that an invisible hand was stroking her hair, and on occasions doors conveniently opened for her as she approached them. But it was during a seance held at the pub that she was to experience her most unusual and frightening experience.

In an attempt to discover the reason for the Wellington's persistent paranormal activity, a Hertfordshire psychical research group who had been ghost hunting for some years were allowed to hold seances in the bar and the cellar. And before long they were able to make contact with what appeared to be the spirit of a lonely little boy.

The tables in the bar were the old-fashioned kind with ornate iron bases and immensely heavy, but during one seance the table where they sat in a circle moved beneath their hands and they saw it rise up right off the floor.

The group preferred to use a rather laborious method of communication with the supernatural, which they believed was most likely to be reliable. Their leader, Fred White, went through the alphabet letter by letter, asking any spirit present to rap after the correct letter, spelling out replies to his questions. Some information could be obtained on the 'one rap for yes, two raps for no' principle, and Mr White often asked for the raps to be made in different parts of the room, or on the floor, making it quite impossible for anyone present to fake the responses.

By patient question and answer they built up a touching picture of a little ten year old boy who once lived in the pub when it was the Blue Boar. He recalled when the stables at the back were full of horses, and his friends who used to play with him there. Touchingly he said, 'I like to play but now I am on my own.' He admitted opening doors for the barmaid Sylvia, and stroking her hair, rapping out 'She is like my Ma'.

But when he asked if he could kiss her, this was understandably an alarming moment for Sylvia who had no idea what to expect. There can be few people who have been kissed by a ghost, or would be able to contemplate the prospect without sheer terror. What was it like?

Sylvia told me that she had bowed her head, heart

beating fast, and waited with tense apprehension for the ghost child's kiss. Then suddenly there it was! A moist, cold sensation on her forehead 'just like an ice cube being pressed there'.

Sometimes during a seance there would be a cacophony of crackling sounds like static electricity, and at times when the ghost had been most active, two members of the psychic research group complained of feeling faint, almost as if their vitality were being drained away.

One evening the group stood in the eerie old cellar, and Fred White asked the ghost 'If he could help us to be aware that he was near us'. Apparently he was, and one by one every member of the circle felt a puff of ice cold air in their faces.

'He doesn't seem to realise that he is dead,' Fred White told me. They had suggested that the lonely little ghost might like to find rest, but he dismissed this, rapping out a swift 'No'. He was quite happy where he was, thank you.

Although most of the supernatural happenings at the Wellington seemed to fit the mischievous but sometimes touchingly lonely personality of a child, the psychical group formed the opinion that there might be more than one ghost there. The replies were at times more mature in character, and one customer who visited the men's cloakroom one day came back in a hurry, really shaken, saying that when he looked in the mirror another man's face had looked back at him.

Naturally, everyone took care not to say anything about the pub's supernatural happenings in the hearing of the landlord's two small children but in any case, aged three and four at the time they would not have known what a ghost was. But from the start they would never go down to the cellar, and they started coming downstairs into the bar in the evenings in search of their parents, complaining

'Daddy, tell that man who comes into our bedroom to go away'.

In the mid 1970s, the owners sold the Wellington and it was converted into a butchers' shop. I sometimes wondered if the little ghost had survived among the new hygienic white tiling and the chops and steaks. So, one day I went there to find out . . .

11

Little Boy Lost (Part 2)

K EVIN didn't expect to find anyone about in the yard when he arrived one dark winter morning. After all, it was only just after half-past five, and a bit early for customers at Matthews' butchers' shop, St Albans, where he worked.

'I was backing up the drive when I thought I saw someone standing there waiting, with his arms folded across his chest. But when I got out of the car, there was no one about at all. It made me feel rather uneasy, as I felt sure I'd seen somebody. But,' he added hastily, 'I'm still not saying I believe in the ghost!'

I had called round at the shop on a quiet afternoon, and was sitting enjoying a cup of tea with Kevin, John, the shop manager, and Jane, the cashier, in the little office at the back. There had been a lot of changes since this familiar old building was the Wellington pub, but apparently one thing hadn't changed. The place still appeared to be haunted.

They told me what had happened to Gary. This young assistant had gone out to the dustbins in the back yard late one afternoon. The light was just fading, and as Gary passed a pile of empty boxes and cartons, to his surprise he saw a hand come up over the top and push the whole lot down on top of him. Naturally he thought that one of the other assistants was playing a joke on him, but he was amazed when he found that there was absolutely no one there, and the rest of the staff were in the shop.

That wasn't Gary's only alarming experience. One day he went down to the cellar to get fresh sawdust, and as he turned round to go he was startled to see the shadowy form of a man close beside him. Dropping the sawdust all over the floor, Gary stumbled up the steep cellar steps and back into the shop, white as his apron and absolutely petrified.

'I went back down there with him,' said Kevin, still playing it cool about ghosts, 'I made him walk all round and have a jolly good look because I just didn't believe it.'

But later much the same thing happened to David, another young assistant. He too had gone down to the cellar, and he was gripped with a feeling of sheer fear when he became suddenly aware of the presence of a small misty figure far too close for comfort.

'I rushed back up,' he said. 'I was really scared. I never believed in ghosts before this, but now I don't know what to think.'

'There are such things as ghosts all right,' said John, the manager. 'All kinds of things happen here. Take our fridges. Normally the meters last for years and years, but they keep burning out here. The radio and the fires are always going on and off for no reason, and we've had to have two fans replaced recently.'

The staff always parked their cars in the yard at the back, and the succession of punctured tyres that had been found ever since the shop opened was really remarkable. I suggested that mischievous boys might be responsible. 'Could be, I suppose,' replied John doubtfully, 'But we've never seen anybody in the yard. I had three punctures in one day recently, which is a bit unusual to say the least!'

'And there's always so much broken glass about,' added Kevin. 'Goodness knows where it all comes from.'

'One morning there was a crate with a dozen milk

bottles outside the back door when I arrived,' said John, 'and there right in the middle was just one bottle completely smashed to smithereens. The others all round it were undamaged. It's difficult to imagine how that could happen naturally.'

They told me about the day a strange acrid smell began to filter through the shop. 'It really choked us, and customers were commenting on it,' said John, 'but we couldn't account for it at all. Then really thick smoke began to fill the shop. We searched everywhere inside and out, but we couldn't make out where it was coming from.'

The door to the office had been shut, but just in case, someone opened it, and even looked inside the small cupboard in there where one of the girl assistants had left her bag. When the bag was opened they found that the inside was smouldering, which seemed quite inexplicable as all it contained was a hairbrush and a spare pair of shoes. There were no matches, or lighter, or anything that could possibly have caused a fire, but this was the only possible source that they could find for all the smoke and the horrible smell, although there was hardly any smoke in the cupboard itself.

Oddly enough, a pillow in a polythene cover lay beside the bag in the cupboard, but it showed no sign of damage, although polythene would be expected to melt in heat.

There seemed to be no logical explanation for this odd happening, and John told me that coats which had been hanging in the room smelt unpleasant for a long time afterwards. And later a large mirror which had been screwed to the wall in the same room was found smashed in pieces on the floor, but the screws which had secured it to the wall were still there in place.

When the building was the Wellington pub, the barmaid Sylvia experienced many of the ghost's unwelcome attentions, and after Matthews' butchers shop took over the premises, he seemed to have transferred his affections to Jane, the cashier. Many times she had the uncanny sensation that invisible fingers were lightly stroking her face.

'It felt like a cobweb,' was how she described it, 'but there was never anything to see.'

Even more unnerving was an occasion when she was working in the office alone, and suddenly heard the sound of someone breathing heavily close beside her, followed by a curious whimpering noise. Soon afterwards, when she went into the girls' cloakroom, the whimpering started again so suddenly and so close beside her that she screamed.

During the conversion of the pub into the butchers' shop the builders noticed that the empty old building they were working on appeared to have something strange about it. There was often the sound of footsteps overhead, and odd inexplicable happenings. They called the invisible presence Fred, and wrote the name in the concrete at the top of the cellar steps.

The cellar, which had seemed far older than the Wellington pub, had been modernised for the butchers' use, but when I went down there with some of the shop's staff it still felt eerie. The walls had been renovated but the feeling emanating from them was ancient – old enough to be part of the old Blue Boar inn.

It didn't help that somehow we couldn't get the lights to switch on! Things like that happened all the time there. And when I accidentally walked into an old coat left hanging up, the shock was almost too much for me!

It certainly seemed as if the long history of haunting was not yet at an end. Since then the shop has changed hands several times. The staff at a gentlemen's outfitters that followed the butchers told me that doors banged unexpectedly, and goods were often moved around, but remembering previous happenings, the paranormal activity seemed to be quietening down. Of course, there were no girl assistants like Sylvia, the Wellington's barmaid or Jane, the cashier at the butchers' to inspire the attentions of the little ghost who still missed his mother.

When the Christopher Place shopping precinct was built there were more changes, and in the course of construction the inn yard and old stables at the back disappeared for ever beneath new shops. It seemed like time for the ghost to finally take his leave as well. But has he?

12

The Strange Will of Henry Trigg

ONE morning in 1964 Mr Fred Usher was busy carrying out some renovations in a building in Middle Row, Stevenage.

'I went into the storeroom for a crowbar when I noticed this old chap coming through the doorway,' he later told a reporter from the local newspaper. 'I didn't really take much notice, as workmen from Mr Smith's engineering firm next door are always coming in and out.

'He must have been about 5ft 8in tall, and I remember that he was shabbily dressed in an overcoat and gaiters. I asked him if he wanted Bob Smith, but he didn't answer, and seemed to drift past me. I turned, and nearly collapsed when I saw him disappearing through the solid brick wall. I had a quick look to make sure there was no one there, then went as fast as I could next door.'

A shaken, white-faced Mr Usher shot into Robert Smith's engineering works, and sat down rather suddenly. 'I told him he looked as if he had seen a ghost,' said Mr Smith, 'and he said "I think I just have!" I don't believe in ghosts or anything, but this makes me wonder as I have known Fred for a long time and I know it really takes something to upset him like that.'

Apparently 85 year old Mr Stan Winter, who used to own the building where Mr Usher had been working, was able to throw some light on the strange happening. He told them that behind the wall through which Mr Usher's mysterious visitor had disappeared lay the barn where

Henry Trigg's famous coffin was placed in the rafters in 1724.

'You've probably disturbed him with all the noise you're making,' Mr Winter calmly told his friend.

After that, none of the men working at Arrow Smith's Engineering Works really fancied being there alone at night in case Henry Trigg paid a return visit.

So who was Henry Trigg, and how has it come about that parties of school children and other visitors arrive at a branch of the National Westminster Bank in Stevenage with the surprising request – 'Can we see your coffin please?'

Henry Trigg was a prosperous 18th century grocer with a fine twin-gabled shop in Middle Row, Stevenage. He was a bachelor with land and property, a church warden and overseer of the parish, in fact a man of some importance. But when he died in 1724 he was the cause of great embarrassment to his family, for his eccentric will was such a nine days' wonder that copies of it were soon selling like hot cakes.

For Henry had made it clear that he had no intention of joining the dear departed in the churchyard, for reasons that will soon be revealed. He left firm directions that his body was to be committed 'to the West end of my Hovel (barn) to be decently laid there upon a floor erected by my Executor, upon the purlin (roof beam) for the same purpose, nothing doubting but that at the general Resurrection, I shall receive the same again by the mighty power of God'.

Henry's heir and executor was his brother, the Rev Thomas Trigg, but the will specified that if Thomas jibbed at this unusual request, everything was to go to brother George, and so on, down through the family. In view of Henry's considerable estate, it seemed only reasonable to Thomas to humour him, and his lead-lined coffin was duly hoisted up into the rafters of the barn behind the shop where it, or rather a subsequent replacement, can be seen to this day.

The tomb may be a fine and private place, but the same could hardly be said for Henry's barn. Through the years a steady stream of curious sightseers have peered up at the large rough unpolished coffin, patched here and there with rusty metal.

There was even a visit from a team from TV's *Nationwide* programme in 1975, but the lights, cameras and TV reporter failed to persuade Henry to put in an appearance for the evening news programme.

In 1774, Henry's house and shop had become the Old Castle Inn, then during the 19th century, several fires ravaged the thatched buildings of Stevenage, but somehow Henry's barn, and the coffin, went unscathed. After 1922 when the inn's licence was not renewed, it became a branch of the National Westminster Bank. And through it all, Henry's coffin remained high and dry in the rafters of the old barn.

Of course, the question every visitor asks is 'Is Henry Trigg still in his coffin?' Certainly if his niece Ann had had her way, Henry would have been decently interred in the churchyard. She had no patience with her uncle's eccentric ideas, and when she died in 1769 she left 40 shillings in her will for the interment, but this was never carried out.

In fact, in 1831 Mr Bellamy, the landlord of the Old Castle Inn decided to open the coffin, and take a look at old Henry, and he reported that 'the hair on the skull of the deceased is in a perfect state of preservation.'

So at least a hundred years after his death, Henry was still safely up aloft in his barn just as he had intended. For the old grocer had his reasons for preferring his own roof tree to the dangers of the average churchyard in those robust days. It was a time when those grisly acolytes of the surgeon were busy in Hertfordshire. The tears were scarcely dry on many a newly buried citizen's grave before the local body-snatchers were busy arranging a speedy resurrection, as Henry had good reason to know.

One night Henry Trigg and a couple of friends were rolling merrily home after an evening at the Black Swan public house, by way of the churchyard. Suddenly they stopped in their tracks. A will-o-the-wisp of light was flickering among the graves, and fearfully they listened to the disquieting noises coming from a new grave. Could their old neighbour, so recently gone to his long rest, be coming back to haunt them?

With many tankards of courage inside them, Trigg and his friends crept nearer. The sight Henry Trigg saw that night not only sobered him, but inspired the plan that has ensured him a place in Hertfordshire history. After all, he wasn't as young as he used to be, and the idea that his body too, could fall into the hands of body-snatchers, and thence to some surgeon's dissecting room, brought Henry out in a cold sweat.

The three friends crept stealthily away. They knew it would be dangerous to accost what he described as 'those unscrupulous vampires'. But Henry Trigg had seen enough, and while there was still time he began planning his famous will. Details of this, and of his encounter with the grave robbers, are contained in a leaflet available at Stevenage Museum.

Alas for his good intentions, Henry Trigg may have avoided the clutches of the 18th century body-snatchers, but his ultimate fate was almost as bad.

Some time during the 19th century, it was noticed that Henry's coffin was deteriorating badly, and a new one, bound with iron bands was made, and Henry was duly installed and returned to his resting place up in the rafters.

But his peace was short-lived. The East Herts Archaeological Society were the next people to pay Henry a visit, and they reported that the coffin contained 'about two thirds of a male skeleton'.

Worse was to come. During the First World War, Commonwealth soldiers were billeted in Stevenage, and rumour has it that they too opened the coffin and took away some of the bones as souvenirs. Rumour also says that they could, for a consideration, be persuaded to part with them, and when poor Henry's bones ran out, they supplemented the supply with the help of a local butcher.

In a letter to a local newspaper, a resident tells how in 1917 she and a couple of Army friends who were on leave went one moonlit night into Henry's barn, and for a lark climbed up into the rafters. Through a hole in the coffin they hauled out what proved to their astonishment to be horse's bones!

A few discreet enquiries at a neighbouring riding school elicited the explanation that Henry's bones had been gone long since, but copies of his will were still selling well at 6d a time, and there could have been a drop in the revenue if word had got round that the coffin was empty.

Sad to say, that is the case today. Henry Trigg's coffin is quite empty. But what of the man who cared so deeply about what happened to his mortal remains. Is it possible that Henry is still around in spirit?

When I was writing this chapter I was told that renovation work was about to start on Henry's barn. It was of course during some previous renovations that Mr Usher had his unnerving experience.

Who knows? It could be that we haven't yet heard the last of the eccentric Henry Trigg.

13

A Ghost
to the Rescue

IT'S odd the things that come into your mind when you're hanging in space, suspended by one hand, with nothing beneath you but a lot of air! For a start, it's no good getting in a panic. At least that's what my friend Ann says, and I'm willing to take her word for it.

Ann has a lot of practical common sense so when she mentioned in a matter-of-fact kind of way that she had just met her first ghost, I was interested. And as it turned out this was no encounter with a shadowy grey lady nor even a headless knight. No, this was quite an ordinary chap as ghosts go, and his name was Joe. At least, that was what Ann called him.

Ann is that fairly rare bird, a woman engineer, and she and her husband had just moved their business to new premises in St Albans at the time. The new place had been a greengrocer's shop for about 60 years, and there was some modernising and redecorating to be done. They had the first floor, and another firm were due to move in downstairs. And that winter, Ann was often there getting on with the decorating on her own.

'It was very cold, and quite damp,' she told me. 'I always seemed to be breaking off to make hot coffee. Sometimes there were workmen in downstairs, and I used to take them a cup too.'

One day, hearing someone moving about on the ground floor, Ann thought 'Poor chap, I bet he's cold too. I'll take him a drink'. So, cup in hand, she went downstairs.

But to her surprise, there was nobody there at all.

This happened several times, and Ann often found that although it certainly sounded as if there was someone else working downstairs, a look round showed that she had the place to herself.

'What sort of sounds did you hear?' I asked her.

'Well, it usually sounded like someone dropping tools – screwdrivers, and things like that.'

Then there were the paint brushes. As every do-it-yourselfer knows, the worst job is cleaning the brushes at the end of a long decorating session. Ann admitted that mostly she gave her brushes a quick wash before dashing off home, and hoped they wouldn't dry too hard by the next day. But often when she arrived at the premises she would find the brushes soft and beautifully clean. Just as if somebody had been doing the job for her! But who?

'I used to say "Good old Joe",' said Ann, for by now she was beginning to take the invisible tool dropper for granted, and had christened him Joseph. All the same, she was relieved to find that her husband noticed Joe too. She had half-expected he'd say she was imagining things.

One day he was up in the loft, trying to push some wire through the wall to put in a power point. 'What I need,' he said, exasperated, 'is a bit of old piping to poke this wire through.'

'Come and have some coffee, and leave it to Joe,' joked Ann.

Afterwards when her husband returned to the loft to try again, he soon reappeared, looking rather pale. He'd found just the right piece of piping lying handy where he'd been working! Whoever or whatever was sharing their new premises was becoming quite a useful addition to the staff!

Then one afternoon Ann wanted to fill in some cracks in the staircase wall before painting it. The only way to reach them was to wedge a ladder from the half-way landing across the stairs. 'It was a crazy thing to do,' she admitted, 'but I wanted to get on with it.'

The cracks were high up on the wall and as Ann leaned to one side to reach them the ladder began to slide. Quickly she grabbed at the banister rail, one foot desperately hooked round the slipping ladder, her other foot treading air! It was an awkward situation because she knew she was alone in the building.

Trying to be sensible about her alarming predicament, Ann realised that she could only hang on for a very short time. And it was a long way to drop. She looked down, and to her surprise and immense relief, she saw there was someone standing at the foot of the ladder. He was a little wiry man with greying hair wearing an old tweed cap and a brown canvas apron of the sort carpenters used to wear.

'You know how a man looks when he thinks you've done something really stupid?' Ann said. 'He shook his head as if to say "Women!" then he pushed the ladder back so that I could get both feet on and climb down. I called out "Thank goodness you were there!" but he didn't say anything, and I saw him walk into the office at the foot of the stairs.

'Naturally I went after him. I just thought he was a workman doing something for the firm downstairs. It was such a godsend he'd turned up then, and I wanted to thank him.'

But the office was empty! Ann had just seen the man walk in there, but now he had apparently disappeared completely.

Thinking it over, Ann concluded that the man had seemed ordinary enough, although perhaps his clothes were a bit old-fashioned. And she had noticed something rather significant. There had been a big hole in the corner of his apron pocket!

'I remember thinking "So that's why he drops all those

tools",' Ann went on. She realised then that the idea that her knight errant could be Joe was already there in her mind.

All the same, Ann is a level-headed woman, and when she next saw the ground floor people she casually mentioned the workman. They looked surprised. They hadn't expected any workman, they said.

When Ann showed me round her compact office and workshop at the top of the old house, the pine walls, coffee emulsion and fresh white paint looked charming. It certainly didn't look much like a typical haunted house.

Ann laughed. 'The other day,' she said, 'we were busy up here when there was this almighty bang on the wall. We thought something had happened downstairs, and my husband went tearing downstairs, and met the man from the ground floor office rushing up! They'd both heard the noise loud and clear, but they couldn't find anything to account for it.

'I suppose we take Joe for granted now like part of the family,' she said. 'He was very noisy the other day and my two sons were dashing up and downstairs here trying to catch him!'

Obviously Joe has a sense of humour as well as a talent for providing a friendly helping hand!

14

The Haunting
of Minsden Chapel

THERE is something about a picturesque ancient ruin
that demands more than crumbling ivy clad stone
walls and a roof through which the birds fly unhindered.
There should be an atmosphere, almost tangible that
suggests to the sensitive visitor that possibly they are not
alone, nor entirely welcome.

Minsden Chapel, a ruin for more than 300 years, is
such a place. As far back as 1650 it was reported to be
in great decay, and before the end of the 17th century it
was 'totally ruinated, stripped, uncovered, decayed and
demolished'. Naturally there had to be a ghost, and
tradition says that there is. It is a phantom monk who
appears on All Hallows Eve at midnight, as the long lost
bells of Minsden toll. The figure mounts steps, long since
vanished, at the north-east end of the chapel, then is seen
to fade to the haunting sound of sweet, plaintive music.

A bridleway leads up through the fields from the Royal
Oak public house near Preston on the B656 road, and
another track runs from the B651 road to the hilltop where
Minsden Chapel stands almost hidden in woodland,
surrounded by a sea of nettles. Within the flint walls lies
a thick stone slab, cracked across and repaired, a memorial
to the man whose name will always be associated with
Minsden, the historian Reginald Hine.

As a young man, Hine often visited Minsden alone or
with friends, and one of them, a photographer, T.W.
Latchmore, produced a wonderfully atmospheric

photograph of the ruins complete with ghostly monk. Was this photograph a clever fake, or did Latchmore secure a rare record of Minsden's hooded spectre? Reginald Hine never contradicted the impression that he believed it to be genuine.

Hine, who loved Minsden, leased the ruins for his lifetime from the church and warned 'trespassers and sacrilegious persons' that he would 'proceed against them with the utmost rigour of the law and after my death and burial, I will endeavour in all ghostly ways to protect and haunt its hallowed walls'. Sadly he died in 1949 in tragic circumstances, and as he wished, Minsden became his last resting place.

It was a labour of love for him to research the history of the place which meant so much to him, and which he included in his *History of Hitchin*.

Built in the 14th century, Minsden was a chapel of ease serving adjoining hamlets, and a place where pilgrims en route for St Albans Abbey could pause for shelter and worship. By the middle of the 17th century it was already starting to decay, but it became quite the fashion for young brides, who found the little woodland chapel charmingly romantic, to insist on having their wedding there with doves cooing in the trees and wild flowers all around.

One can imagine the comments of guests on the days when rain dripped through the roof or they shivered in their wedding finery as a stiff breeze blew through the dilapidated walls. Even worse, when the occasional lump of plaster or stone fell on the heads below!

It was in 1738 at the marriage of Enoch West and Mary Horn that a piece of masonry fell, knocking the prayer book out of the officiating curate's hand! The Bishop decided that enough was enough, and no more weddings were allowed in Minsden Chapel.

The chapel deteriorated fast as local entrepreneurs

helped themselves to lead, oak beams and stone. The bells, whose ghostly echo is now said to herald the appearance of Minsden's ghost, were found to be missing in 1725, by curious coincidence after someone with a horse and cart was seen driving rapidly away from the chapel one night. And as for the stained glass windows, it seems that they were looted too, as some windows of 'painted glass' were known to have changed hands at the Sun Inn in Hitchin.

Elliott O'Donnell, a well-known ghost-hunter of his time, wrote to Hine that he and some friends visited Minsden chapel one All Hallows Eve hoping for a glimpse of the ghostly monk, but the visit turned to farce when the local policeman apprehended them, thinking they were poachers. Undeterred, O'Donnell undertook another visit alone, when he said he 'felt extraordinarily uncanny at times. I was conscious of something close beside me, scrutinising me, although I neither saw nor heard anything'.

And in spite of yet another visit when he and his friends were the target of practical jokers, he said he was inclined to think there was truth in the legend of the Minsden ghost.

Peter Underwood, President of the Ghost Club, visited Minsden one morning and thought he heard the faint sounds of music which had no obvious origin, but when he later spent the night of All Hallows Eve there, he saw 'a white cross which seemed to glow with an unnatural brightness for a few seconds before fading and then reappearing a few seconds later'. He thought it could possibly have been a trick of the moonlight, but he did feel conscious of a presence.

Hine himself who spent a lot of time at Minsden, both by day and night, said he had never heard or seen anything supernatural.

When I visited Minsden last year I found that someone

had made several small bonfires there surrounding the trunk of a young tree inserted in the ground with bunches of fading wild flowers tied to it. Was it just a May Day lark by local youngsters or, as it was the time of Beltane, could it have had some connection with a witchcraft ceremony? I'm sure Reginald Hine, who regarded himself as the guardian of Minsden Chapel, would not have approved.

Apart from that, I felt that Minsden had a serenely peaceful atmosphere with nothing eerie about it. But then, it was a sunny May bank holiday afternoon. Midnight on All Hallows Eve would be a different proposition, and for a ghost hunter with sufficient nerve, a much more likely time for an appointment with Minsden Chapel's mysterious ghostly monk.

15

The Return
of The Saint

AROUND 1870 a young couple, Henry and Emma
Toulmin, rented the Gorhambury dower house from
Lord Verulam. It was called The Pre, a long white
Georgian house with a verandah at the back, the garden
running down to the river Ver, and beyond were the fields
where once the Roman city of Verulamium stood.

Henry and Emma were delighted with their new home,
especially the number of bedrooms, as they expected to
have a large family. They already had three children, and
eventually the family would number 14, eleven girls and
three boys, although one beloved son died young.

Their second daughter Mary began to write the story
of her family when she was twelve, and her enchanting
book *Happy World* was revised and published under her
married name, Mary Carbery, in 1991 by Longmans,
Green and Co. In it Victorian Hertfordshire is reflected
through the fresh eye of a child. Instead of grave sepia
tinted strangers from a dusty photograph album, there are
human beings, very much alive and kicking, and as real
as ourselves, and her fresh and lively accounts of Victorian
St Albans, Harpenden races, and the country life and
customs are full of delight and humour.

A trip into St Albans was a treat, where the friendly
old town crier in his blue coat with silver buttons would
lift the children down from the carriage. Mary always
bought a silk Bible marker complete with text from the
Penny Bazaar, but the shop lady would shake her head

as she handed over yet another, as she thought such a love of texts in one so young meant that Mary was not long for this world. The butcher next door would pop his head round the corner and ask 'Not at it again?' and then urge Mary to eat plenty of underdone beef to make her strong. 'You stick to beef and give texts the go-by miss,' was his forthright advice.

When Mary was older, a trip to the town with her German governess would include a quick secret expedition to the coffee tavern in French Row where they hurriedly consumed hot sausages and coffee.

But an outing with Mary's mother was more likely to be through alleyways and back yards to visit the poor, such as old Miss Skeggs and her seven cats. The old lady loved to talk about the wonderful day she saw the ghost of 'The Saint' when she lived in Verulam Road, and he was so bright and shining that she had to wear an eye shade over her dazzled eyes ever afterwards. No one ever saw her without it.

At that time Mary did not apparently know that a member of her family was also there when this extraordinary apparition appeared, or that one of her sisters would one day experience a similar vision. Isobel was very much younger, the 13th child born into the large Toulmin family, and it was as a very old lady nearly 20 years ago that she recalled the shining figure she saw one summer night in the garden of The Pre when she was 16.

One of her sisters was ill, and Isobel had run out into the garden to chase away a cat that was causing a disturbance. It was peaceful and lovely in the garden that evening, and then suddenly, beyond the tall garden hedge, she was entranced to see a figure in white, about twice the height of a man, shining in a haze of beautiful golden light.

'It was quite motionless and perfectly lovely,' she was

later to recall. 'It stayed absolutely still for about three minutes and then, as I turned to call to another sister who had followed me into the garden, it vanished.

'All the time I watched it the figure seemed to be in a shimmering robe of white. It was the vision of a man with a golden radiance about his head and shoulders, and this gradually enveloped the whole figure. I was only sixteen on that wonderful night, and I kept very quiet because of my sister who was sick. I feared that it might be interpreted as an omen.'

Later on, longing to tell someone about her experience, she wrote to her older brother Henry, who was in America. He wrote back, telling Isobel that he too had once seen 'The Saint' and sent her a drawing illustrating just what he saw.

'When I looked at it I had the sensation that once again I was close to that radiant figure on the Verulam Road,' she said.

Henry told Isobel that he too had been there when Miss Skeggs had her sighting of 'The Saint with a glory round his head'. She lived in tiny Rats Cottage on the Verulam Road then, long since demolished, and as well as Isobel's brother Henry, Miss Skeggs' vision was shared by the Toulmin's family butler, Mr Bolton, who was passing by at the time.

In Mary Toulmin's book she refers to Miss Skeggs's vision as the ghost of St Amphibalus. Amphibalus, a fugitive priest, was sheltered by Alban, who was almost certainly an Anglo-Roman citizen of Verulamium. Taken captive after helping Amphibalus to escape, Alban declared his new Christian faith, for which he was beheaded and became the first Christian martyr. So there is the possibility that her 'Saint' was Alban rather than Amphibalus.

There is another possibility. At Mold in Wales there

was a barrow called Bryn-yr-Ellylon, or Fairy Hill, long reputed to be haunted by the ghost of a figure in shining golden armour. The barrow was opened in 1832 and the skeleton of a tall man was found, wearing a garment of bronze overlaid with gold, indicating a person of some importance. This cape, now in the British Museum, is believed to date back many centuries B.C.

In 1992 an archaeological dig in the grounds of St Albans City Hospital, a short distance from Verulamium and the Pre, uncovered the site of a Roman temple and the grave of a Celtic ruler.

There were signs that this grave was the resting place of a member of a royal family, possibly a king of the Catuvellauni tribe whose capital was Verlamio, in what is now Prae Wood, within sight of Pre House. The tribal king there at the end of the first century BC was Tasciovanus, father of Cunobelin, Shakespeare's Cymbeline, and he is a possible occupant of the Celtic grave, now once more buried beneath a new housing estate. So could Miss Toulmin's ghost have even been Tasciovanus or a member of his family?

The remains of twelve oxen and of three skeletons, possibly human sacrifices, were found, also horse harness of bronze and enamel, and the remnants of chain mail. Unfortunately nothing like the golden garment found at Mold was discovered, but time for the dig was limited as the land was required for building.

Isobel Toulmin believed that the vision of 'The Saint' had been seen at rare intervals during the history of St Albans, so there is always a possibility that it may yet reappear.

Years after the Toulmin family spent their idyllic childhood at the Pre House, their old home became a hotel. Not surprisingly perhaps, people have sensed something in the atmosphere that suggested echoes of the past. People who occupied one particular bedroom mentioned quick footsteps in the passage outside and taps on the door, but there was never anyone to be seen.

There is yet another quite unusual ghost story associated with the Pre Hotel. Many wedding receptions took place there, and the lovely garden was a favourite spot for photographs. When some of the pictures of the bride and groom were developed, something odd appeared. There beside them was the shadowy figure of a child. A member of the staff of those days recalled the first time it happened.

'The young couple had posed on the lawn just below Room 15,' she said, 'and when the photograph was developed, there was this extraordinary outline of a small child. No one could explain it. There were no children in the wedding party or among the guests at the hotel.' And subsequently the same little figure appeared on other wedding photographs, usually in the month of August.

When Isobel Toulmin heard about this, she was convinced that she herself was the shadowy child in the pictures. 'If there is a powerful affection for a place, I am sure a living person can project the ghost of their earlier self,' she said, explaining that she never liked strangers on the lawn in the garden she loved so much.

This may of course be the explanation. There are many examples of the ghosts of living people being seen.

The Pre Hotel has now become a popular Beefeater restaurant and hotel. Nevertheless it has been the setting for some very unusual supernatural happenings. And possibly may be again.

16

'. . . And Battles Long Ago'

MANY hauntings have a story behind them involving tragedy and emotions so powerful that they appear to have left some kind of paranormal record that can sometimes become apparent to those who come after. And surely battles must be the most likely events to have imprinted themselves on the very atmosphere of the sites where they once took place.

Indeed it is a matter of historical record that shortly after the battle of Edgehill in 1641, a ghostly re-enactment was seen in the sky one night by a group of shepherds and other terrified spectators.

They hurried to inform the local minister, who with a magistrate accompanied them the following night to the battlefield where, to their utter astonishment and alarm, the whole spectacle was again re-enacted. And the following weekend 'the same tumults and prodigious sights and actions' were once again seen.

King Charles was told about this extraordinary event, and sent several of his officers to question the witnesses. And again, on the following Saturday and Sunday they too were able to see the spectral battle, and even recognise their own friends who had taken part and been killed.

The battle of Marston Moor in 1644 also left echoes behind of a less spectacular kind. In November 1932, a commercial traveller and his companion were driving across Marston Moor en route for Harrogate. It was a typically misty November night, and in the car's headlights they could see some men ahead of them.

They reported afterwards that the men wore long cloaks, top boots or leggings, and over their long hair they had large brimmed hats turned up at one side with cockades. They presented an unusual sight in such a place, but the driver's main concern was to avoid running into them as he passed an oncoming bus. Both bus and car dimmed their lights as they passed, but when the car headlights were turned up again, there was no sign of the group.

The two men in the car were so surprised that they stopped and looked round, but the road was quite deserted and there was nowhere they could have gone. The area, and the men's strikingly unusual appearance has been taken to suggest that what the motorists had seen was a group of weary warriors from the battle of Marston Moor.

The battle of Sedgemoor in 1685 was short but terrible in the carnage inflicted by King James II's forces on the supporters of the Duke of Monmouth, the illegitimate son of Charles II. In the folklore of Somerset there are stories of ghostly sightings of phantom soldiers and horsemen in flight from the battlefield, their weapons and uniforms clear enough to be identified.

But it is on the night of the 6th July, the anniversary of Monmouth's defeat, that people have seen Monmouth himself, his cloak flying, riding hell for leather away from the battlefield. There have been many witnesses to this sighting of Charles's ill-starred son, en route for his capture and execution on Tower Hill soon afterwards.

St Albans was the site of two of the most important battles of the Wars of the Roses. The Clock Tower still stands as it did in 1455 when the first Battle of St Albans raged round it, and King Henry VI's forces met with disaster.

An ancient building called Battlefield House once stood

in Chequer Street where modern shops are now, but some of the fiercest fighting is said to have taken place around there and the Abbey Green close by, and periodically the sound of galloping horses, shouts and the clash of steel have been heard in the area, although nothing is ever seen.

The second Battle of St Albans took place in 1461 on Shrove Tuesday, 17th February. Margaret of Anjou, King Henry VI's dominating wife, brought her Lancastrian forces down from the north en route for London, and the powerful Yorkist, Warwick, brought 30,000 men out to St Albans to confront her before she could reach the capital.

He had four days grace to prepare, and his forces were arranged in sections, on Bernards Heath, St Albans, in the Sandridge Valley and on No Mans Land, too far apart for close liaison. Warwick's preparations involved large cord nets intended to check infantry charges, and protective wooden screens for archers and artillery men who were expected to fire through holes.

His forces included swordsmen, men with handguns, archers and cannoniers firing stone shot, and with all the latest equipment in place Warwick's set piece awaited the Lancastrian forces.

According to plan, a strong force of archers took immediate toll of the forefront of Lancastrians as they arrived in St Albans, and they rapidly diverted, coming up Folly Lane and Catherine Street to St Peter's church and on to Bernards Heath.

Alas for Warwick's well-prepared position. After their long wait, Warwick's men were taken by surprise and attacked from behind. They were heavily outnumbered and as they struggled gallantly against overwhelming odds, snow fell on a terrible scene of carnage and defeat. The survivors fled in disarray, and Warwick was ultimately left with about 4,000 men out of his proud army of 30,000 and forced to retreat.

But while Queen Margaret and King Henry gave thanks for victory at St Albans Abbey, the city suffered a night of riot and terror at the hands of Margaret's plundering hordes, and when word of this reached London the outraged citizens closed their gates against her. And Edward, son of the Duke of York, was able to return to London in triumph to become Edward IV.

Bernards Heath is a stone's throw from my own home, and from time to time while exercising my dog there I have picked up small completely round stones, and idly wondered if they could be stone shot from the battle.

One day I had a curious experience there. As I walked towards the wooded part of the Common I noticed something odd about the trees. They were completely still, with no movement in the leaves and branches, appearing to resemble a painted back drop, and everywhere seemed unnaturally quiet. I walked on into the trees and suddenly all hell broke loose. I could feel movement, violent movement, all around me. I felt that horses were rearing up almost on top of me, and I could hear neighing, shouts and the clash of metal so close that I threw my arms over my head to protect myself from I knew not what, as there was absolutely nothing to see.

As I whirled round to get away, there in front of me with his back to a tree sat a man. He was wearing a leather cap and jerkin, boots and some sort of leggings, and he had bow and arrows. He was holding his head in his hands and I could tell he was wounded and in pain.

As I looked at him he began to fade, and I realised I could see the trunk of the tree through him, and seconds later he had vanished.

Somehow I found myself out of the trees with the feel of the breeze on my face, and the sound of birds and the traffic on the Harpenden Road just as usual. My dog came running towards me and we walked home, as I tried to come to terms with what had happened, and find some rational explanation for it. Nothing like that has ever happened again, and I visit Bernards Heath often, but I have never forgotten the day when I really believe I may have walked into a re-enactment of part of that Shrove Tuesday battle so long ago.

17

Last Post for a Villain

A T the side of the Bull's Green to Bramfield Road on the edge of woodland is one of Hertfordshire's curiosities, a stout wooden post carved with the words CLIBBON POST, and the date 28.12.1782. It is there to mark the final resting place of a man whose reign of terror in that part of Hertfordshire ended violently in the woods there one cold winter's day in 1782.

Walter Clibbon and his three sons were well known at Hertford market and country fairs where they sold pies and cakes, and were on familiar terms with the neighbourhood farmers. But Walter, the pieman dressed in his smock and bearing his tray of goodies, was not what he appeared to any local Simple Simon. In reality the Clibbons were a family of tough criminals, and even Mrs Clibbon would dress in men's clothes and join her husband and sons in their nefarious activities.

Weaving his way among the busy crowds at the market, or keeping an ear cocked in the local hostelries, the wily Clibbon could unobtrusively listen to the gossip about who had done well that day, and select the unsuspecting victims he and his family would attack and rob as they made their way home. With their faces disguised with soot, the Clibbons went unrecognised, and no one made any connection between the familiar pieman and the vicious robber who parted many a farmer from his hard earned money, and savagely beat him up into the bargain.

On the 28th December 1782, a young Datchworth man

called William Whittenbury was held up and robbed as he came through the woods at Oakenvalley Bottom, near Bull's Green. William knew better than to take on his assailants, but he went straight to nearby Queen Hoo Hall where his uncle Benjamin Whittenbury lived, and they returned to the woods with Benjamin's servant, Shock North, taking a gun. The robbers were still there, waiting for their next victim, and there was a terrific fight, in which the Whittenburys were soon getting the worst of it.

Benjamin Whittenbury was knocked down, and thinking his last hour had come, cried out to his servant, 'Shoot Shock, or I'm a dead man'.

Shock fired, killing the father, Walter Clibbon. One son managed to escape, but another was captured, and after being charged at the Assizes, was later hanged.

Walter Clibbon's body was taken to The Horns public house at Bull's Green, where he and his sons had often stopped for a drink. It was kept in a shed overnight, and the next day people flocked there to see the stiff, frozen body of the villainous pieman.

Feeling against the man who had deceived and robbed many of them was running high, and although Clibbon was dead, a desire for vengeance inspired some of the locals to tie the corpse to a horse and set it galloping along with the body bumping along behind it. According to a contemporary account 'they dragged it up and down the Green and through the furze to their heart's content, and when satisfied, they took it back to the Horns' outhouse'.

It was generally agreed that Clibbon should not be given a Christian burial in the churchyard, and it was decided that he should be buried in the woods where he had been shot.

And so at the side of the road between Bull's Green and Bramfield they buried Walter Clibbon, the renegade pieman, and drove a stout wooden post through his heart,

97

with an inscription which read:

> Here continues to rot the body of Walter Clibbon, who
> with his sons robbed and ill-treated many persons in
> this neighbourhood. Please do not deface this.

The gun with which Shock North despatched Walter
Clibbon was put on show at Hertford Museum, and the
Lord Lieutenant of the County presented a cup to
Benjamin Whittenbury inscribed 'In recognition of his
spirited behaviour in risking his life in securing Joseph
Clibbon, the son, and having been instrumental in
shooting Walter Clibbon, the father, a most notorious and
inhuman offender'.

The post, or one of the subsequent replacements, still
marks the spot. Locally, superstitious residents believed
it would stop the pieman's ghost walking.

But did it? There are stories that evening travellers in
the area have seen the shadowy shape of a horse pulling
'a black writhing body' along the lanes. Others have heard
the sound of horse's hooves and the scattering of gravel,
and unearthly groans.

If indeed some events are so powerful or emotionally
strong that they leave an impression that people coming
afterwards may be able to sense, could it be that the spirit
of the black-hearted pieman is still re-enacting his awful
end?

18

The Death of a Witch

PEOPLE came running into the streets at the sound of the trumpets. After all, it wasn't every day that a splendid troop of the Royal Horse Guards came galloping through the Hertfordshire countryside. But who was the pale, grim faced man riding with them?

'That's Thomas Colley,' the murmur went round. 'The one who murdered old Ruth Osborne. They're going to hang him at Gubblecote Cross.'

Some followed after to be in at the death. There were those who thought that Colley's fate was just retribution for his diabolical crime. Others thought it hard that a man should hang for ridding the community of a wicked old witch. And yet others kept their guilty thoughts to themselves.

For many a man, uneasily remembering the happenings of 22nd April 1751, just four months earlier, watched Thomas Colley go by on his last ride, and thought with shame, 'There but for the grace of God . . .'

The death penalty for witchcraft had been abolished in 1735, but in country districts old superstitions and beliefs were far from dead. And John Butterfield, then the landlord of the Black Horse pub at Gubblecote, had never forgotten the time he had fallen foul of old Ruth Osborne.

He had been a dairyman then, and Ruth had come to him one day asking for buttermilk. He had to refuse because he needed all he had for the pigs, but she had taken his refusal badly and gone off grumbling.

Not long afterwards he had fallen ill with what seems to have been a form of epilepsy. And as if that wasn't enough, his calves were ailing. John Butterfield cast about in his mind wondering who might feel ill-will towards him. When he remembered the time Ruth Osborne had been so put out about the buttermilk, his suspicion grew that the old woman must be at the root of his troubles. For sure, Ruth Osborne must have bewitched him.

Well, set a witch to catch a witch, they said. He consulted a wise woman from Northamptonshire who at once scented witchcraft at work. But the charms she used had little effect, and John Butterfield had carried a grudge against old Ruth ever since.

It seems that local feeling was aroused as a result of his claims, and in the market places of Hemel Hempstead, Leighton Buzzard and Winslow on an April day meant for better things, the town criers proclaimed 'This is to give notice that on Monday next, a man and woman are to be publicly ducked at Tring in this county for their crimes'.

One of those who stopped to listen was Mr Burton, the overseer of the poor at Tring. And when he found that the man and woman concerned were two harmless old people he knew well, John and Ruth Osborne, he realised that there was no time to be lost. He took the Osbornes into the workhouse for their own safety. But Burton had not reckoned on the size of the riotous mob which arrived on 22nd April in an ugly mood. They began smashing windows and battering the workhouse walls, and the Osbornes were hastily smuggled out and locked in the church for safety.

Insatiable in their determination to find their victims, the rioters, led by Thomas Colley, a chimney sweep, swarmed into the workhouse, turning it upside down in their search. And when they could not find the Osbornes, in their fury they threatened to burn the place down, finally forcing the master of the workhouse to reveal the old people's hiding place.

The Osbornes were hauled off to the pond at Long Marston, where stripped naked, with thumbs and toes tied together and wrapped in sheets, they were thrown three times into the water to sink or swim. 'Swimming' a witch was a recognised test. It was believed that a witch could not sink, and when Ruth Osborne appeared to float on the surface, Thomas Colley, the self-appointed master of ceremonies, mercilessly poked and prodded her under with a stick every time she struggled to get her head above water.

It was a long and cruel ordeal for two people in their seventies, and Ruth was left on the bank in her wet sheet while their tormentors ducked her husband, and then dragged her across the pond again with a rope. She did not survive, and the doctor who examined her body said that she had died partly by being suffocated by mud and water, and partly through exposure. Her husband was taken to a nearby house, more dead than alive, and he too, died soon afterwards.

The heartless Colley had lost no time in taking a collection from the crowd for his efforts, but the forces of justice were soon hot on his heels.

The savage mob of witch-hunters had soon melted away, but someone had to pay for that diabolical day's work, and that someone was the ring-leader, Thomas Colley. He was tried at Hertford assizes before Sir William Lee, found guilty of murder, and sentenced to be hanged.

And so on 23rd August 1751 Thomas Colley left Hertford escorted by 108 men of the Royal Regiment of Horse Guards, seven officers, and two trumpeters. He lodged the night at St Albans jail and next day they took him to Gubblecote Cross, near Long Marston, where he was hanged and his body then hung in chains and left to swing for many years afterwards as an awful warning.

As for Ruth Osborne, many secretly believed that she really had been a witch. The pond where she met her miserable end was said to have been in a field off Astrope Lane, Long Marston, an area local people avoided after dark for fear of meeting Ruth Osborne's ghost.

People did not forget Thomas Colley either. No one lingered near his gibbet after dark, for the place acquired an uneasy reputation. Some said it was haunted by Colley's ghost in the form of a dog with burning eyes. A huge dog it was, and black – black as a sweep.

19

Ghosts
of Old St Albans

ST Albans has been in the path of history since the earliest times, and the heart of the city, where many old buildings have a story to tell, is full of memories. Those who take the Ghost Walk organised by St Albans City Guides find that almost every few yards there are haunting tales of grey ladies, monks and walled up housemaids!

The picturesque medieval Gables in Market Place, now Laura Ashley, once housed Boots the Chemists, where an assistant once saw the ghost of 'an evil looking man' by the fireplace in the upper floor. Another wraith seen in the upper part of the building is an old lady sitting by the window, apparently making pillow lace, and assistants working in the shop avoided visiting that storeroom on dark afternoons.

The adjoining building, once part of the Gables, was converted into a separate shop some time ago, and one of the people getting the shop ready used to take his small son with him. The child was running about upstairs, laughing and talking, and when asked what he was doing replied 'I'm playing with the man up here'.

I have written at greater length about the old Wellington pub which was opposite the Gables, but passing along Market Place we reach W.H. Smith, the newsagents. This building was the ancient Moot Hall, where the trial of those taking part in the Peasants Revolt took place in 1381. The staff call their ghost Henry, a fairly harmless character who likes to switch the lights on and off.

The Grange is a handsome building in the centre of St Peter's Street, a stone's throw from the Alban Arena, the city's main centre of entertainment. Mayor John Osborn built the Grange in 1763, and his daughter-in-law, Dorothy, is said to have committed suicide there, for reasons lost to us but thought to concern an affair of the heart. It was used as council offices from 1940 and many employees were unnerved by the alarming appearance of a grey lady drifting about the premises. The then town clerk, Betty Entwistle, decided the ghost must be Dorothy Osborn, and council employees tried to avoid working late on their own as this was the time when the grey lady was likely to put in an appearance.

The new city hall, now called the Alban Arena, was built on the area that once was the garden of the Grange, and Dorothy sometimes takes a stroll there in the wee small hours. Muriel Thresher, who conducts the Ghost Walk, told me, 'She always wears a grey silk gown, and is seen with a luminous aura of light around her.

'One night after a mayoral banquet in the hall, the caretaker was waiting to lock up. Everyone else had gone, but he had noticed a lady in a grey dress go into the powder room, so he waited for her to come out. Well, he waited, and he waited, and in the end he went in, and there was no one there.'

Another splendid building, Ivy House, was built for himself by Edward Strong, who was Sir Christopher Wren's chief mason during the building of St Paul's Cathedral. There lingers a pathetic little servant girl who haunts the main staircase, still industriously carrying out her duties. Her tragic story is that she worked in a house that was formerly on the same site, and after some misdemeanor, was walled up in a chimney.

Cleaners say the cellar never needs cleaning and the

staircase handrail is always highly polished. A former branch manager went back to the office to collect some papers one night in 1975 and told the local paper, 'It was dark and windy and as I went through the front door I saw a figure in white standing on the stairs. It appeared to be a young woman with blonde hair. She gave me a cursory glance and then disappeared up the stairs.

'I fled from the building and told my wife, who was waiting in the car, that I had just seen a ghost. Now I think twice about going to the office after dark.'

Nevertheless, he and his son went there later, just after Christmas, to remove a Christmas tree from the entrance hall. There was no one else in the building, but they suddenly heard approaching footsteps, and left in a hurry!

Another unhappy servant was a butler, caught drinking his master's brandy. The shame of it caused him to take his own life, and his ghost was seen in 1977. He had previously put in an appearance in 1872 when his white wigged apparition in silver buttoned livery drew a crowd of 200 when he appeared at the window of Mallinson House, St Peter's Street.

Not far away at the Pemberton Almshouses, founded in 1627, one resident describes how sometimes when she comes back after shopping she finds her neatly made bed has the distinct imprint of a large body, and the room reeks of strong tobacco.

Her unseen visitor doesn't worry the old lady at all. 'I always say Come out, come out, wherever you are,' she laughs, 'but he never does!'

In St Michael's Street on the fringe of the town one of St Albans oldest restaurants is the historic Sally Lunn. The ghost of a lady in white often seen around the restaurant and on the stairs is believed to be a former owner keeping tabs on how her business is being run.

In 1986 an assistant at the restaurant reported, 'She was

just sitting on a bench when I went upstairs. She looks about 45 and was dressed all in white.

'I wasn't frightened, but I think that's because I believe in ghosts. I think it is Sally Lunn, keeping an eye on the place. A few times afterwards I had the feeling I was being watched or there was someone else in the room, but I've not seen her since.'

A former chef who saw the ghost late one night about six years ago wasn't so happy about it. He turned white with fright, and ran out of the restaurant, never to return!

The estate agents Strutt and Parker of Holywell Hill, take quite calmly the presence of apparitions in their 14th century offices. Being so near the Abbey with its Benedictine phantoms, they are not fazed to have their own wandering monk on the premises, and also a Cavalier soldier, who has been seen sitting by the fireplace, amiably smoking his pipe.

A department store called Fisks once stood in the High Street and was haunted by the ghost of a corsetiere who committed suicide after being crossed in love. Girl assistants sometimes saw her wandering around and a display of wedding veils and head-dresses was often found upset. Obviously weddings were a sore point with the lady who never had her own. Prayers for her soul were said to help her find peace, but when Fisks was demolished and new shops were built on the site, there were still problems.

A wallpaper and paint shop experienced poltergeist activity and sometimes found their goods thrown around in the mornings, but at a hairdressers' salon close by it was just the opposite. Used towels that had been left in a heap were found neatly folded!

Hertfordshire has its share of Roman soldiers still marching through the countryside hundreds of years after their companions left. But it was a solitary Roman centurion which terrified a local inhabitant as he walked home through Verulamium one night in 1985. As the figure rode towards him on horseback, the young man ran for his life. Unfortunately in his haste he fell, hurting himself and ending up in Casualty.

And other Roman visitors have been seen not far away in houses in Kingsbury Avenue and Camlet Way, thought to be the site of a Roman cemetery.

The list goes on: nuns, First World War soldiers, coaches and horses, shadowy gardeners; the echoes of the past seem particularly loud and clear in St Albans where the Ghost Walk must surely soon become a Marathon!

The Watford Hauntings

SO many theatres are haunted that one must assume that sitting in comfort watching the latest production has considerably more appeal for the average phantom than roaming the chilly corridors of some unheated stately home, or the crumbling battlements of a ruined castle.

Theatre ghosts, like Drury Lane's famous Man in Grey, or the Victorian actor William Terriss who haunts the Adelphi theatre and Covent Garden tube, met their deaths in tragic circumstances, and still seem to be earthbound in the same area.

The Theatre Royal at York identified their Grey Lady by holding a seance and found that she was a 17th century novice nun; she was subsequently exorcised. Bath Theatre Royal's Grey Lady who occupies a box is supposed to have committed suicide after her husband discovered her liaison with an actor and killed him in a duel.

There are many other theatre ghosts, and actors generally believe that a sighting denotes good luck for the production.

Watford Palace theatre also has its own ghost story which is said to have its origins in the early days. The theatre opened at the end of 1908 with a full programme of singers, dancers, comedians, acrobats and 'a panoramic exhibition of animated pictures' which the proprietors proudly advertised as 'such as to be found in the Metropolis, without the inconvenience of an irksome Railway journey' and promised that the performance would be full of fun, frolic and instruction. Who could ask for more? Especially since the cheapest seats cost only fourpence, and wealthy patrons could lord it in a box for 10/6d.

For many years it was a variety theatre where most of the well-known music hall stars of the day appeared before it changed over to repertory. Jimmy Perry, of *Dad's Army* fame, who managed the theatre for some years in the 1950s and 1960s, told me that in the early days performers would do a turn at the old Metropolitan music hall in the Edgware Road and then get a fast pony and trap to Watford to do another show at the Palace.

Old playbills show that Marie Lloyd, Gracie Fields, Nellie Wallace, George Robey and many other old-time stars performed at the Palace, and even Charlie Chaplin came in 1912 with Fred Karno's Mumming Birds before Hollywood claimed him.

It may have been about this time that tragedy struck. When I made enquiries at the theatre I was told that in the early days a female follow-spot operator fell from the gallery to her death below, and subsequently became the Palace's 'resident spook'.

Stories of the ghost they call 'Aggie' are part of the history of the theatre, and the last known sighting was when an usherette was locking up the gallery after an evening performance. To her alarm, she noticed that a ghostly figure was walking along the back of the gallery, and as she watched, it continued down the aisle and 'leapt over the barriers', leaving her considerably shaken.

Backstage staff have sometimes sensed an unseen presence, and heard footsteps that could not be accounted for. An empty theatre can be an eerie place, with an auditorium full of echoes and dark shadows. Sometimes work on scenery and stage sets must be done when the stage is available, maybe late at night.

On one such occasion, when a new set was being erected in the early hours of the morning, members of the staff were disturbed to see curtains covering a door fluttering to one side as though someone was walking through them. And they watched mesmerised as footsteps then progressed across to another door where the same thing happened the unseen presence apparently pushed aside the curtain there and passed through.

Jimmy Perry told me that he never saw the Watford Palace ghost himself, but he understood that she was a dresser at the theatre who was in the upper circle or gallery when she fell to her death.

Whether Watford Palace's ghost was a follow-spot operator or a dresser, her sad fate seems in no doubt, and although it is some time since anyone has seen her, this is yet another theatre with one member of the staff who never goes home.

Not far away from the theatre in Watford's busy High Street is an Elizabethan building with an appropriate ghost, a Tudor gentleman in doublet and hose seen many times when the upper floors were occupied by Copperfields restaurant.

Despite its modern hustle and bustle, Watford's history spans the centuries. Mr Albert Fiedler who used to own Copperfields until about three years ago, and encountered the ghost several times, told me that people from English Heritage examined the building and declared it to be definitely Elizabethan, and the lower area is believed to be even older. It was the type of residence that might have belonged to a wealthy merchant, with living quarters on the upper storey and possibly a shop on the ground floor, with a yard and stables at the back.

The ghost did not put in an appearance immediately after Mr Fiedler took over the premises. In fact it was a few years before he had his first encounter with what may well have been the building's earlier owner. 'I was in the kitchen one day,' he told me, 'and I had the impression there was someone in the restaurant so I went out to speak to them, and that was when I realised that what I was seeing wasn't a real person. It was more like a grey mist.

'It happened so quickly. I felt sure I had seen some-one, or something, and then I found myself wondering afterwards if I had really seen anything or not. Or was it just my imagination?'

One day soon afterwards, when the premises were closed, one of the girls who worked in the kitchen went into the restaurant and seconds later Mr Fiedler heard her scream. She rushed back in a state of shock, insisting she had seen something out there in the restaurant, and nothing would induce her to go back.

'I went out there, but there was nothing to be seen,' said Mr Fiedler. 'I hadn't mentioned to any of the staff that I had seen anything previously, so I asked her just what she had seen. She described it as a grey shape that moved across the restaurant.'

A few months later when Mr Fiedler went into the restaurant after closing time he saw at once that the ghost he had seen previously was out there, and this time it appeared to have a much more definite shape.

'I saw this character quite clearly, although it didn't appear to have any colour. It was in shades of grey, not at all misty, but more like a black and white television picture.

'The dress he was wearing reminded me of pictures of Sir Francis Drake. He had a tight fitting tunic with puffy sleeves and a collar or ruff, short trousers and sort of leggings. He was very short, only about five foot tall I should think. He appeared to be an old man, and he had features but they were very difficult to determine.'

There were other sightings. Some time later the girl who had screamed when she saw the ghost went into the restaurant but she came back immediately, very distressed, and said she had seen it again. Mr Fiedler asked her to describe what she had seen, and her description tallied closely with his own sighting.

And on another occasion, Mr Fiedler's father-in-law was sitting in the restaurant waiting for him and he too, saw the small Tudor figure pass through the room. 'I had never told him what I had seen previously,' said Mr Fiedler, 'but he described the same apparition.'

When the Copperfield ghost appeared, it seemed to come up the staircase and move across the lower level of the restaurant, which is the oldest part of the building dating back to the 15th century. Then when it reached the outside wall it disappeared.

Although seeing the ghost unexpectedly was rather an unnerving experience, Mr Fiedler felt that it was friendly and not at all frightening, but understandably none of his staff who had seen the spectral Elizabethan would have cared to spend the night alone in the building.

One member of staff, Ivy, had worked on the premises for previous owners for at least 15 years before Copperfields came. She was aware that the building was haunted, and said that although she didn't actually see anything, she sometimes felt she was in communication with an unseen presence. She had the impression that someone had spoken to her and would find herself answering before she realised that there was no one there.

Mr Fiedler said: 'Sometimes I would hear her and say "Who are you talking to, Ivy?" And she'd say "I was talking to the old man, he's around again". She was a rational, sensible person, not inclined to imagine things, and at that time I hadn't mentioned that I had seen anything myself.'

The restaurant area is now offices, and when I spoke to staff they told me they had only been there for a few months. They agreed that this interesting old building had a very strong feeling of the past but they had not been visited by the Tudor ghost.

It was only a month later that Diane, one of the staff, telephoned. She sounded tense and apprehensive.

'I was working late when I suddenly had this feeling of tension in the pit of my stomach, and although I didn't see anything, I just knew the ghost was there. There was something in the atmosphere that was very strong, stronger than anything I've ever felt before, and I just had to get away.

'It was an indescribable feeling. I could sense a change in the atmosphere, and although I couldn't see him, it was as if he was trying to communicate with me. We have recently had new security alarms fitted and I felt he was unhappy or angry about them. I found myself apologising to him as I set them before leaving.'

It needed a strong effort of will for Diane to go into another room to get her coat, as any moment she felt she might actually see the apparition, and as she ran out to her car she felt badly shaken.

When I spoke to Diane's colleague Wendy, she said that she often got into the office early and quite often she thought someone called out 'Good morning'. Instinctively she answered, only to find that she was the first to arrive! This was reminiscent of the experience of Copperfield's employee, Ivy, who usually got to the restaurant in the morning before everyone else, and had the distinct impression someone had greeted her. She would casually reply 'Morning', and then find she was alone.

Both girls said that since moving into the offices there had been trouble with the computers, and all kinds of things had mysteriously disappeared. The new alarms had all gone off together for no reason and it had been impossible to stop them for some time. All these happenings might have a reasonable explanation of course, if it had not been for the strong sensation that, as Ivy used to say, 'the old man is around again'.

One of Watford's other ghosts is a little younger than the Tudor gentleman in the High Street. Jack O'Cassiobury was a negro slave in the 18th century, owned by a wealthy woman whose property skirted the Grand Union Canal as it passed through Cassiobury Park. This grand lady found the presence of the waterway so close to her own grounds extremely distasteful, so it was Jack's job to harass the men on the coal barges as they passed through Ironbridge Lock.

Jack was strong and as agile as a monkey, tormenting and attacking the men and causing as much chaos as possible by leaping upon them when they least expected it. But one day he went too far and met his match. One of his victims swung out at him in a fury and taken off guard, Jack was knocked senseless and fell into the canal. The bargees went on their way satisfied, and Jack was left to drown.

Ironbridge Lock was no longer the scene of the daily harassment of bargees by their lively tormentor, but before long there were stories that gave the place a sinister reputation. It was somewhere to avoid if possible for fear of a frightening phantom, the still agile ghost of Jack O'Cassiobury. And still is!

21

Stranger on a Train

CAN the spirits of the dead sometimes return to the aid of the living? There are stories of occasions when some disaster has been averted by the timely intervention of someone not of this world, and one of the most dramatic events of this kind which happened on a train passing through Hertfordshire, was reported in the *Hertfordshire Express* on 17th March 1894.

This is the Great Northern Railway driver's own account of what happened on a day he would never forget.

'Three years ago I was driving the 8.30 train to the North, and left Kings Cross four minutes behind time. I can't tell you what it was, but I never felt nervousness but once on an engine, and that was on the night I'm talking about. I don't know nothing about ghosts or spirits, or apparitions – call 'em what you like – but I'm ready to swear before any judge today that I saw something of the kind that night, and no amount of argument will change my belief.

'It was just when we were passing through Hatfield when, I would take my oath for all I am worth, a man stepped from the platform to the footplate, just as easily as though we weren't travelling about 55 miles an hour. Aye, I can see his face and dress to this day. It was the saddest face I ever come across. The eyes seemed to look you through and through, and when on top of that I saw he was all in black, I never was so afraid in my life.

'The curious thing is that Dick, my fireman, saw

115

nothing of it. He coaled up for the hill by Welwyn just as natural as though all was fair sailing, and when I tried to shout to him I felt a great lump in my throat, and not a word could I speak.

'I soon noticed that the strange-comer never went to any other part of the footplate except to the spot whereon I stood, and he even hedged up so close to me that I went cold all over and my feet were like lumps of ice.

'I think I must have acted mechanically, for I watched the man put his hand upon the regulator, and I put mine on with him. The touch of it was like the touch of snow, but I couldn't loose it, and before I knew what I'd done, the steam was cut off and the train was slowing.

'Dick, I know, thought I was mad. He'd been away on the tender, breaking up the coal, but he came down and craned his neck when steam was off, and he saw, as I saw, that the distant signal was off, and after that the home signal stood for line clear.

'You won't believe, perhaps, but its Gospel truth, that although I knew the way was right, I was compelled to stop the express, and stop her I did outside Hitchin Station.

'For nothing you say? Well, Heaven alone knows how, but it proved to be for a great deal. There were two trucks across the main line, and although the signals were off, the way was blocked, so that me and the passengers behind me wouldn't be living to tell the story if I hadn't been compelled to pull up as I did.'

Hertfordshire has one other railway story concerning the time the new railway line to the north was being made by the LNER Company in the mid-19th century. Near Watford, the construction workers were obliged to bore a tunnel through an old churchyard with gruesome results as broken coffins and bones came to light and sometimes fell down on to the workmen. But the work had to go on, and eventually the steam locomotives were roaring through on their way to the north.

But all was not well. It happened that the boilers usually needed firing as they reached the tunnel, and the locomotive plate men found that at this particular place there would be a dangerous 'blow-back' and a number of engine drivers were seriously injured by the flames.

When the problem was investigated it was found that the trouble always happened as the engine passed below the old graveyard and, not surprisingly, it was superstitiously believed that the spirits of the dead were expressing their anger at the disturbance they had suffered.

22

A Ghost at
the Grocers

TWO ancient roads, the Ickneild Way and Roman
Ermine Street intersect each other where once the old
Royston Cross used to stand, and close by is Royston's
unique curiosity, a mysterious underground cave of great
antiquity, its chalk walls decorated with primitive figures
of kings, queens, warriors and saints. Who created it,
when and for what purpose, has fired people's imagination
ever since workmen discovered it by chance in 1742.

James I had a palace at Royston, and often came to
hunt in the ancient forest and beautiful open countryside.
It was while at the palace that he signed the warrant
that sent Sir Walter Raleigh to the block, and James's
Witchcraft Act had dire consequences for two Royston
women who were accused of dabbling in the black arts.

A bloodcurdling history of curses and dark doings
eventually brought Johane Harrison and her daughter
Anne to trial at Hertford, where the evil powers and
familiar spirits they claimed to possess could not save
them, and they were put to death. A gentler soul was
Henry Andrews, an 18th century Royston schoolmaster
and astrologer. For 45 years his predictions made *Old
Moore's Almanac* a top seller, interest in what the stars
foretell being just as keen then as now.

Surely a place like Royston must have ghosts, and
certainly there are old stories to chill the blood, but many
have more shadow than substance on closer examination.

There is the spectral lady seen in the area where King

James's hunting lodge used to be, still tending her long vanished garden. And they say disembodied footsteps echo at night through the modern shopping arcade, Angel Pavement, where once the haunted old Angel pub stood.

At a High Street hairdressers sawn-up bones were once found under the floor boards of what is known as the Tudor Room. There are stories of sudden chilling drops in temperature and a grey lady who is heard but not seen by those who work in the offices that have replaced the hairdressers.

In 1992 there were strange happenings at the North Star pub. New landlords had just taken over, usually a signal for any pub ghost to make a special effort to be noticed. Many small objects like keys disappeared and turned up in unlikely places, locked doors were found mysteriously open, and when the locked cellar was opened in the mornings, the lights would be on. The gas taps for the beer in the cellar were tampered with, and a full ice-making machine was found switched off and inexplicably empty.

Whatever the cause of the unnatural activity, the landlord's pet Alsatian was aware of it. He howled miserably, and would rush out of the room, his hackles raised in terror. Upstairs they heard odd tapping noises and felt icy cold currents of air. And even worse, a terrible smell enveloped the bedroom at times.

When I enquired, I found that the landlords who suffered these alarming manifestations had moved on, and apparently there have been no recent incidents of this kind. Remembering a similar saga at the Wellington pub, St Albans, which continued unabated for many years, perhaps the North Star has been lucky.

Royston's best known haunting has persisted for a long period in an old building at the top of the High Street. Part of it is now occupied by a shoe repairers and there

I was shown a wooden plaque over the inside of the front door. The words 'Grosvenor Elston, Purveyor of Wines and Spirits' relate to a mysterious former owner of which little appears to be known, but who is believed to be at the root of the odd happenings that have disturbed the building.

The story is that Grosvenor Elston hanged himself in the cellar of his shop from a large hook which is still there, and his unquiet spirit is still earthbound in the premises that once were his. It was during the years that the shop was occupied by the grocers A.E. Baker & Co that the manifestations were at their height. These were typical of poltergeist activity with goods thrown off shelves on to the floor, or unaccountably moved from one place to another.

When the manager arrived for work in the mornings, he often found groceries moved from their usual positions, and even heavy items such as large tins of biscuits had been transferred elsewhere. The staff heard the sound of footsteps overhead when there was no one in the upstairs rooms, and on one occasion a member of the staff had the unnerving experience of encountering a shadowy 'something' on the stairs. She had walked right through it before she realised!

There were not many actual sightings but on one occasion a man's figure was seen in a corner by someone living in the flat upstairs. Several times there was the unmistakeable noise of bottles rattling in the empty cellar, as if they were being moved about, and once a stand holding cider bottles in the shop appeared to be lifted up and put down again, making all the bottles clatter together. And that familiar sign of a haunting, the sudden noticeable coldness as the temperature drops for no apparent reason, happened many times.

A.E. Baker & Co occupied the shop for generations, and afterwards Rolph's Garden Supplies were there for some time. The firm have now moved to a modern building opposite, and Richard Rolph, who insisted he was sceptical about ghosts, admitted that members of his staff were convinced their old shop was haunted. No one liked the thought of going down to the cellar, or working late as the atmosphere was so spooky. Mr Rolph stayed late one night to do some painting after the staff had gone home. It was very quiet in the empty building, and he was increasingly aware of a strange atmosphere around him. He ignored his own uneasiness as long as he could, but eventually the uncanny feeling became insupportable.

'All the hairs pricked up on the back of my neck,' he said, 'and I was out the door as quickly as possible.'

Oxfam used the premises for a time, and with all the comings and goings of a busy charity shop the staff had no time to worry about supernatural happenings. But apparently they did notice how often their goods were found in a jumbled heap or scattered all over the floor when they arrived in the mornings. Each shift blamed the other's untidy ways but it seems likely that who or whatever used to move the groceries about at Baker's was up to the same tricks.

At the shoe repairers everyone seemed to know about the shop's reputation, but they were not aware of anything unusual happening in their time.

If all those shoes haven't tempted him, perhaps Grosvenor Elston has moved on at last!

Index

Abbots Langley   23-27
Adrian IV, Pope   23
'Aggie' (Watford Palace
  ghost)   109-110
Alban, St   12,88
Albanus Mass   14, 15
Amphibalus, St   88
Andrews, Henry   118
Angel Inn, Royston   119
Ayot St Lawrence   45-47

Barnet, Battle of   35
Berkhamsted   59
Bernards Heath   93-95
Bishops Stortford   48-53
Black Lion Inn, Bishops
  Stortford   48
Blue Boar Inn,
  St Albans   61, 71
Boadicea   57, 58
Boars Head Inn, Bishops
  Stortford   48
Bonner, Bishop   48,
  49, 52
Bramfield   96, 97
Breakspear, Nicholas
  (Pope Adrian IV)   23
Brocket Arms, The
  45-47
Bryn-yr-Ellylon barrow,
  Mold   89
Bull's Green   96, 97
Burnham Green   57

Cassiobury Park   114
Castlereagh, Lord   30
Catuvellauni, The   89
Chaplin, Charlie   109
Chaplin, Ralph   41
Charles I   91
Charles II   35-36, 52, 92
Child ghost   61-72
Christopher Place,
  St Albans   61, 72
Churchill, Winston   36
Civil War, The   34,
  40, 57, 91-92
Clibbon, Walter   96-98
Cock Inn, Bishops
  Stortford   52-53
Colley, Thomas   99-102
Copperfield's Restaurant,
  Watford   110-114
Cornwallis-West,
  Jenny   36
Cromwell, Oliver   40,
  57, 59
Cross Keys Inn,
  Harpenden   17-20

Dad's Army   109
Datchworth   57, 96
Duse, Eleanora   36

East Herts Archaeological
  Society   77
Edgehill, battle of   91

Edward IV   94
Edward VII   36
Elizabeth I   28
Elston, Grosvenor
   120-121

Fayrfax, Robert   14, 15
Ferrers, Lady Katherine
   39-44
Frith, W.P.   29
Furze, The Revd
Michael, Bishop of
   St Albans   25

*Gazetteer of British
   Ghosts*   24
George Inn, The, Bishops
   Stortford   51
Gerish, W.B.   14, 31
Ghost Club, The   84
'Ghost Walk, The',
   St Albans   103, 104,
   107
Gresley, Sir Nigel and
   Lady   34
Grey Lady, Bishop's
   Stortford   48-53
Gubblecote   99, 101
Gwynn, Nell   35-38,
   52

Hagdell, Harpenden   21
Handscombs Store,
   Bishops Stortford
   49-51

Happy World (Mary
   Carbery)   86
Hare, Augustus   43
Harpenden   17-22
Harpenden Hall   21
Harrison, Johane and
   Anne   118
Hatching Green   21
Hatfield   115
Haunters and the Haunted
   (Lytton)   29
Henry VI   93, 94
Henry VIII   15, 35
Hertford   96, 98, 101
Hine, Reginald   82-85,
Hitchin   58, 83, 84,
   116
Hoddesdon   56
Home, Daniel
   Dunglas   28-29

Ironbridge Lock   114

James I   118
James II   92

Kensworth   43
Knebworth   28-32

Latchmore, T.W.   82
Letchworth Gate   56
London Colney   34
Long Marston   101, 102
Lunn, Sally   105, 106
Luttmann, Willie   15

Lyde, Sir Lionel 45
Lytton, Sir Edward
  Bulyer 28-32 *passim*

Mardleybury Manor
  55-56
Margaret of Anjou 93-94
Markyate 39-44, 56
Marston Moor, battle
  of 91, 92
Matthews' Butchers,
  St Albans 69-71
Mee, Arthur 22
Melba, Dame Nellie 36
Minsden Chapel 82
Monmouth, Duke of 92
Much Hadham 56

Nomansland 39, 41,
  44, 93
North Star Inn,
  Royston 119

O'Cassiobury, Jack 114
O'Donnell, Elliott 84
Old Castle Inn,
  Stevenage 75
Old House Café, Bishops
  Stortford 51-52
Old Moore's Almanac 118
Osborne, Dorothy 104
Osborne, Ruth 99-102

Packhorse Inn, Markyate
  56

Palace Theatre, Watford
  108-110
Pemberton Almshouses
  105
Pendley Beeches 57, 58
Perry, Jimmy 109, 110
Pre, The 87-90 *passim*

Radiant (Yellow) Boy
  29-31
Raleigh, Walter 118
Rees, Eric 19
Revett, Nicholas 45
Rhodes, Cecil 48
Rose Cottage, Harpenden
  20
Rothamsted 17, 21, 22
Royston 118

Saffron Walden 49
Sedgemoor, battle of
  92
St Albans 11-16, 35, 36,
  61-72 *passim*, 78, 83,
  89, 101, 103-107
    Battles of 92-95
St Lawrence's Church,
  Abbots Langley 23
Salisbury Hall 33-38
Shaw, George Bernard
  45
Silver Cup Inn,
  Harpenden 20-21
Spinning, Jenny 31
Stanbridge 59

Stevenage 73-77 *passim*
Strong, Edward 104

Tasciovanus 89
Terris, William 108
Tissiman Stores, Bishops
  Stortford 51
Toms, Dr Elsie 16
Toulmin, Isabel 87-88,
  89, 90
Toulmin, Mary 86-87,
  88
Treble, Mary Ann 23-27
Trigg, Henry 73-77
Tring 57, 59, 100

Underwood, Peter 24,
  84

'Valley of the
  Nightingales' 17-22
Verulamium 86, 88, 89,
  107

Ware 42
Wars of the Roses, The
  35, 92-94 *passim*

Warwick, Richard Neville,
  Earl of, 'The Kingmaker'
  35, 93
Watford 108-114, 116
Waytemore Castle 48-49
Weatherhead, Ann 21
Wellington, The,
  St Albans 61-67, 68,
  70, 71, 72, 103, 119
Welwyn 116
Wheathampstead 58
White, Fred, psychical
  research group 65, 66
White Horse, The,
  Burnham Green 57
Whittenbury, Benjamin
  97, 98
'Wicked Lady, The'
  39-44
Wigginton 57, 59
William I (The
  Conqueror) 48
Woolmer Green 55
Wren, Sir Christopher
  104

'Yellow Boy, The' 29-31